Leading from Where you Are delivers that really explains how to be a *Nurturing Ideation* is applicable to entrepreneurs pitching their idea to investors as well as to startups trying to build their companies. The *Power of Enthusiasm* chapter is brilliant - effectively using a positive mindset. *Leadership Sustainability Ideas* should be printed and laminated for everyday reference.

Kate Klimow, Chief Administrative Officer
and Director of External Relations
University of California, Irvine
Beall Applied Innovation

Leading from Where You Are provides 7 sets of behaviors that will improve your leadership regardless of your role or the organization that you are in. David Coffaro thoroughly grounds these principles in the research literature (he was a student of Peter Drucker), and in his extensive experience in a variety of leadership roles. In addition, he is a marvelous storyteller, so you will be engaged and entertained on your journey toward your personal leader development. Ron Riggio, Ph.D., Henry R. Kravis Professor of Leadership and Organizational Psychology, Kravis Leadership Institute, Claremont McKenna College.

Ronald E. Riggio, Ph.D., Henry R. Kravis Professor
of Leadership and Organizational Psychology
Kravis Leadership Institute, Claremont McKenna College

I've known Dave for several years and have seen him successfully role model each of the seven themes he describes in *Leading from Where You Are.* Dave outlines easy-to-understand leadership themes and practical applications to develop the next generation of leaders at our organizations. Leaders from every sector will benefit from reading this book and reflecting on how their leadership choices and behaviors are making a positive impact on the mission of the organization and the future leaders who work there.

Nicole Suydam, President & CEO
Goodwill of Orange County

I had the good fortune in my consulting career to see Dave Coffaro in action as a leader. I respect him greatly and I am so glad that he has written *Leading from Where You Are* to share with us his experiences. The lessons on Proactive Relationship Management and The Power of Enthusiasm were powerful reminders to me along with each of the key lessons. Dave uses his vast experience to bring each of these lessons to life in a vibrant manner that helped energize my ongoing journey to be humble leader making an impact.

Tommy Marshall, Executive Director,
Georgia Fintech Academy

Dave Coffaro has written a 'how-to' guide for developing and increasing your influence as a leader in an organization. I found the actionable advice at the end of each chapter to be a practical way to put each competency into practice. Best of all, you can read the chapters in any order giving you time to focus and practice one competency at a time before returning to the book for the next one.

Veronica Duluk, Chief Operating Officer
of Private Wealth Management, Wells Fargo

Dave Coffaro's *Leading from Where you Are* is a tremendous guide for every reader to understand, optimize, and contribute their unique, God-given leadership skills to the world. Very insightful and highly readable. The specific, actionable five steps at the end of each chapter is particularly very helpful

Erik Davidson, DBA, CFA
Adjunct Professor of Finance
Baylor University

Leading from Where You Are

7 Themes to Make a Meaningful Impact in Your Work

David Coffaro

Leading from Where You Are
Seven Themes to Make a
Meaningful Impact in Your Work

© 2020 David Coffaro
All Rights Reserved
Published by SACG United States

ISBN: 978-1-7344099-0-1

Contents

Foreword

By Alex Parker
Chief Marketing Officer and Executive Vice President
Redline Detection, LLC

Leading from Where You Are is an operation manual for professionals. Never before have I read a business book with this rare combination of value for authenticity paired with clearly actionable steps designed to help the reader, wherever they may be in their career, to take the role of leader. Dave Coffaro's artful storytelling, paired with concise, easy-to-follow action steps, will have you leading your team with passion and purpose and enjoying every minute. The author distills a wealth of wisdom into smart, modern, bite-sized steps that will turn you into a leader in your organization and the master of your own career.

This book is an action plan to live your best professional life with more authenticity, enthusiasm and intention. Full of funny and engaging stories, the author distills wisdom from a pantheon of greats, Peter Drucker to Mick Jagger, in an enjoyable read that will move you to action. Dave delivers a wealth of value by defining the often elusive action steps to move readers to become authentic, compassionate, enthusiastic and effective leaders.

As a woman in manufacturing, it took a decade of my career to understand how to bring my authentic self to leadership in a traditionally male-dominated field. I recommend *Leading from Where You Are* to every professional, this book will guide you to bringing your best, most authentic self, your highest skills, talents, creativity, empathy and enthusiasm to your professional life, and help you to lead from where you are today.

This modern business book is a life-changing guide for professionals to define their personal brand, write their value proposition narrative, competently and enthusiastically move into leadership in their organization and their lives.

Introduction

Every day, people make thousands of decisions affecting their lives, from relatively simple, and in many cases unconscious, choices – *how hot should the water be before I step into the shower this morning* – to more meaningful decisions like *how do I invest my time during the day, who do I spend time with,* or *what do I believe.* Of these thousands of daily choices, according to Columbia University decision researcher, Sheena Iyengar, the average American makes about 70 *conscious* decisions, a miniscule proportion.

I've anchored this book on one key principle: *leadership is a set of conscious choices and behaviors, not a job title.* Regardless of your specific role in an organization, you can make a meaningful contribution to the enterprise's success, which will fuel your success. Use your voice to shape the organization's direction by *Leading from Where you Are.*

Apply the seven themes discussed in this book in detail, a *practitioner's guide* to leadership, to make your impact as a leader.

A set of foundational assumptions underlay this principle:

- Your *contribution* to the organization of which you are a part is the cornerstone of success in your work. It doesn't matter if you work for a mom and pop business, a 250,000-employee company, a private enterprise, a publicly held corporation, a nonprofit, or a government sector employer. Regardless of the organization type, your value to the enterprise is based on the contributions you make.

- Your contribution is not simply the time you put in at work. It comes from giving of yourself through your skills, talents, abilities and ideas. The value of your contribution increases the less commoditized it becomes. Unique ideas are more valuable contributions than basic skills.

- Engagement in your work begins with a simple question: What can I contribute through my actions today? Of course, you work to earn compensation for your efforts. But, as much research has shown over the years, compensation isn't the primary source of *fulfillment* from work. One recent study showed that 9 out of 10 people would choose to earn less money to do more meaningful work.[1] A strong thread connects meaningful work, engagement, and fulfillment, which comes from feeling you're making a meaningful contribution to your organization, you're engaged, your work is valued and appreciated, and your efforts matter.

- The seven themes defined in *Leading from Where you Are* provide a framework to enhance your contribution to the organization you serve. When you consider leadership a set of choices and behaviors, not a position, questions arise like - *what choices can I make, and actions can I take to demonstrate leadership and optimize my contribution to this organization?* These seven themes will

---

[1] 11/6/18 Harvard Business Review article by Shawn Achor, Andrew Reece, Gabrielle Rosen Kellerman and Alexi Robichaux

help answer these questions and provide you with specific, actionable take-aways you can put into practice now to begin *Leading from Where you Are.*

- In general, the more extraordinary your contribution in your work, the greater the rewards. Those rewards may manifest as recognition, compensation increases, titles, promotions or new opportunities which lead to more fulfilling work.

You'll note that a number of these foundational assumptions center around *contribution, engagement* and *service.* That may feel odd or misguided, but the rationale is sound. When you operate from the question - *what can I contribute* - you position yourself to make a meaningful impact. Success in one's career arises from making a series of meaningful impacts over time. While knowing *'what's in it for me'* is important, that is an outcome, not the starting point.

Academic definitions of leadership center on the action of leading a group of people or an organization. Leadership expert Warren Bennis said, "Leadership is the capacity to translate vision into reality." Management guru Peter Drucker wrote, *Leadership* is "doing the right things." (in contrast to *Management,* which is "doing things right"). These and a great many other definitions describe what leadership *is.* I've focused this book is on *how to practice* leadership from whatever role you play in your organization. These seven themes form a framework to guide you in your leadership journey.

Understanding the 7 Themes

Many people, particularly those early in their careers, are challenged with how to show-up in their work – how to be valuable, influential and supported in their endeavors. This book discusses seven specific themes that help you choreograph your presence in your work.

These seven themes, Proactive Relationship Management, Mastering the Art of Inquiry, Nurturing Ideation, Merchandising Knowledge, Making Strategy Matter, Defining Your Story and The Power of Enthusiasm, will guide and empower you to consciously determine how to make a positive impact and build the value of your personal brand within and beyond your organization. Chapters describing each theme include a set of ideas on how to put the concept into practice. Regular practice of these themes leads to development of new leadership habits which will inform the way you show-up in your work.

Chapter 1
Proactive Relationship Management

I don't consider myself a football fan. The list of things I'd rather do than watch a game on television is extensive. But a few years ago, I heard a football-related story that captured my attention.

Los Angeles has long been a sports town with a large constituency. National Football League football was the main event. In 1946, the Rams relocated from Cleveland, making L.A. the first West Coast city to host an NFL team. When the city lured the Raiders south from Oakland in 1982, L.A. became one of only two cities in the U.S. to host two NFL teams.

For a decade, the fans loved and supported their two professional football teams. The teams and their owners saw a different side of the story. Both teams grew frustrated with their aging stadium, the Los Angeles Coliseum, considered state of the art when it was built in 1923. The city built the iconic stadium as a tribute to World War I veterans. Over the years it hosted USC and UCLA football, Dodgers baseball from 1958 to

1961, the 1959 World Series, Super Bowls I and VII, and the 1932 and 1984 Summer Olympics games.

As the years passed, the Rams and Raiders watched new modern stadiums built in far smaller cities than L.A., and grew frustrated with their outdated venue, which they saw as an impairment to growing and sustaining their fan bases.

They watched many attempts to stimulate development of a new football arena in the L.A. area. All failed. By 1994, the teams saw no visible progress and started listening to proposals from cities hungrier for a new stadium and an NFL team than L.A. appeared to be. Out of frustration, both teams from the City of Angels elected to abandon their hometown. Oakland lured the Raiders back to their old home and St. Louis enticed the Rams with a new stadium and a hungry fan base.

That Christmas Eve, in the closing game of the 1994 season, the Rams lost to the Redskins in what became the final NFL football game of the twentieth century played in Los Angeles.

For the next twenty years, rumors of the possible development of a new sports arena to attract an NFL team back to Los Angeles swirled. Hopes rose as story after story about an arena project emerged, followed by the disappointment of learning the rumor had no substance.

Everything changed on January 5, 2015, when the owners of the Hollywood Park Race Track in Inglewood, adjacent to Los Angeles, announced a partnership with Kroenke Sports & Entertainment to build a multi-purpose 70,000-seat stadium designed for the NFL. The new state-of-the-art arena included 260 luxury suites, 13,000 premium seats, and over three million square feet of usable space, with an original estimated price tag of $2.6 billion. This massive investment would create the world's most expensive sports arena. The proposed project required many levels of approval before it could come to fruition.

One day while the Inglewood city council considered the new stadium project, I sat in my car and listened to a reporter on a local Los Angeles news station discuss plans for the new arena.

She said, "This is a huge, multi-year project with a very large price tag. Developers tell us the new arena would be good for the city, the local economy and would become another highly visible landmark attraction in the L.A. area. But not everyone is excited about the plans."

Then she spoke with a city council member with a very different point of view. He said, "We can't just blindly jump into this kind of a commitment without knowing all the risks. Right now, we don't even know for sure if we'll have an NFL team to play here. Some cities have gone down this path and ended up stuck with a money pit on their hands and a bunch of unhappy taxpayers who got strapped with the bill to cover unexpected expenses."

The council member continued through a litany of potential problems with the proposed project, sparing no detail. Finally, as the story concluded, he said, "I didn't hear about this project until plans were already well under way. If they would have included me in the conversation from the beginning, maybe I could have helped avoid some of the potential problems and pitfalls that are likely to come up."

The councilman's words were important, but his *message* struck me. On the surface, he urged caution and diligence before moving forward with a new stadium project. At a gut level, I heard how it *felt* to be excluded and infer your opinion doesn't matter.

I don't know if other city council members inadvertently missed the importance of engaging with this councilman or if their actions were intentional. Regardless of the cause, failure to develop allies has consequences. I imagined the unspoken part of the message, *"You want to get something done in my jurisdiction, but, because you didn't respect me enough to get to know me and hear my thoughts, I'm going to make you understand just what a big mistake you made."*

The councilman's reaction is not unique to politicians. Being on the outside looking in never feels good. Human beings are social creatures who want to be part of relationships, part of the conversation, part of success. Yet, relationships don't happen automatically. It takes a *conscious effort* to make real, person-to-person connections. This chapter focuses on how to intentionally, proactively cultivate professional relationships to benefit you and your organization.

Your ability to engage, communicate and influence others correlates with the quality of your relationships.

Effective relationships are essential to success in our work. Every business is a people business, comprised of individuals who value professional relationships. In a high energy organization where expectations border on unrealistic, you may feel like only *tasks* matter. Similarly, with people working remotely or as independent contractors, you can unconsciously create the perception that relationships are less important than tasks.

Solid relationships animate task performance. When others feel connected to you, they will collaborate with you. This doesn't mean all professional relationships are equally relevant; they're not. How another person's work or role intersects with your work determines relationship relevance, which is why Proactive Relationship Management is a foundational ingredient in *Leading from Where you Are.*

A recent article in Inc. magazine described the qualities of a "rock-star" employee as integrity, proven ability to get things done, low drama, no surprises, and passion. The article left out the common view that rock stars earned their title as solo artists, accomplishing great feats by themselves.

This idea of extraordinary individuals succeeding alone dates to long before modern day rock stars entered the scene.

One explanation of leadership from the 19th century, the Great Man/Great Woman theory, says important events in history are attributable to the impact of great individuals with extraordinary innate characteristics like outstanding intellect, heroic courage, or divine inspiration.

In 1841, Scottish philosopher Thomas Carlyle published *On Heroes, Hero-Worship, and The Heroic in History,* where he brought forward the idea that the history of the world is but the biography of great men, the heroes who *singularly* impacted the path of history.

We know today that it takes a village to accomplish great things. An extraordinarily gifted individual cannot produce extraordinary results without the engagement of others working towards common objectives. This reality is true even for *real rock stars.* People like Ed Sheeran, Taylor Swift or Lady Gaga have extraordinary talent, yet still need effective relationships with people across a range of stakeholders to do what they do successfully.

Consider the relationship management required for a rock star to take their show on the road. I read about a recent worldwide concert tour that started in Europe, traveled to the U.S., then moved to Asia for the final series of concerts.

The tour manager talked about the logistics of producing the show in each venue. His organization sounded more like a multinational corporation than a rock band on the road. A production manager led the transportation crew, tech team and roadies who did all the load-in, set-up, and tear down of equipment. The location team worked with site-specific vendors and unique location requirements. An advance person handled pre-arrival arrangements for the crew and performers. A stage manager ran all support tasks necessary during performances. Add in the sound crew, lighting crew, back line crew, truck drivers, bus drivers, airplanes and pilots and on and on.

The take-away is that even real rock stars are not solo acts; they are part of an *interconnected ecosystem where trusting relationships are essential to their success.*

Making time to invest in relationships

I first met Carl while I waited with him for an elevator around noon at the bank headquarters where I worked. Carl wore a Greg Norman shark-embroidered golf shift, khaki pants, and Ferragamo-looking loafers. He sported a great tan as if he'd just stepped off the course at Pebble Beach.

From a quick glance, I assumed he wasn't a banker – no obligatory pin-striped suit. Must be stopping by to visit someone he knew that worked at headquarters, I guessed. I noticed he carried a bag from the sandwich shop next door, so perhaps he was taking lunch to a friend who worked at the bank.

Before the elevator arrived, he said, "I'm not sure we've met. Do you work for the bank?"

At that point, I believed he was a client, maybe trying to find someone who worked in the building. I said, "Yes, I do work here. My name is Dave." I reached out to shake his hand.

When the elevator arrived, we both stepped into the car and hit the buttons for our respective floors.

He hit the button for the top floor, said, "I'm Carl. I've been around this place for a while, but I don't always get to know everyone at the bank right away. How long have you worked here?"

His question intrigued me. The company had close to 60,000 employees, with 500 working at the home office, so I knew his comment about not getting to know *everyone* was a subtle way to start a conversation.

I said, "I've been with the company about a year, but I only spend a couple of days a week at the home office."

Carl said, "Next time you're in town, why don't we get a cup of coffee together. I'd like to get to know you and hear what you do at the bank."

I later learned Carl was a long-tenured senior executive with the bank. His resume included time in every major division of the company, and the CEO viewed him as the guy who could figure out how to make anything in the company work better.

I took Carl up on his invitation to visit over a cup of coffee, and over time, had the good fortune of getting to know one of the most interesting, engaging people I've ever worked with. I learned that he *never* wore a suit to work at the bank! Six months after we met, the management in my division changed and Carl became my boss.

Carl was a cool character – a bright, creative and inspiring leader. Even more valuable than those characteristics, Carl had strong relationships with people at all levels throughout the bank. I don't know how many people he met while waiting for an elevator, but I do know he developed relationships with colleagues in most departments of the company, including some areas I didn't know existed.

Carl exemplified proactive relationship management. He initiated relationships and found reasons to stay in contact with people. As a result, Carl made friends and knew subject matter experts across the company who he could turn to whenever he had a question or wanted a different perspective on an issue.

In an ideal world, colleagues come to you, reach out their hand and *invite* you to get to know them. Carl was an exception. In the real world, that doesn't happen often. The responsibility for proactivity falls fully on you to *Lead from Where you Are*. With this acknowledgement of responsibility, the question becomes - *how do I proactively engage and with whom*?

Creating time to develop relationships may sound ridiculous. Who has *extra time* in their day to focus on relationships? One of the most effective strategies in managing time is to prioritize highly beneficial activities like proactive relationship initiation and engagement. When you consciously allocate time in your day for *intentional outreach* to colleagues, you tell them you're interested in them and want to understand what matters in their work. Intentionally commit time on your calendar every week to Proactive Relationship Management to give yourself space to get to know people whose paths cross your own.

Carl's invitation to get a cup of coffee together is one way to start a relationship. A new connection can also begin through a brief face-to-face meeting with a subtle purpose, like asking a colleague how a project they're working on is coming along. It could take the form of blocking time on your calendar to have lunch with a co-worker you interact with occasionally and want to know better. The take-away: Intentionally prioritize Proactive Relationship Management as part of your standard operating procedure.

From my experience with Carl, I learned to block time on my calendar every week to develop and expand relationships with co-workers, team members, clients, prospects, vendors and other stakeholders who fill my priority relationship list.

I've found that initiating contact to begin or continue a relationship is a powerful tool to expand connectivity in my work and enhance my influence. I make relationships the most important assets in my business. I know they are critical in your work as well.

Owning your calendar and time blocking

One of my favorite Peter Drucker books is *The Effective Executive*. Though written in 1966, the lessons remain as applicable today as when the book was first published. The overriding message is that you can learn effectiveness – *doing the right things*.   A foundational step to enhance one's effectiveness is to *know thy time*.

Per Drucker, effective executives don't start with their tasks, they start with their time. They don't start with a plan, they start by finding out *where their time goes*, then attempt to manage their time to make the greatest possible impact through their work.

Everyone has the same number of hours available every day, yet some people are extraordinarily effective in how and where they invest their time while others, in Drucker's words, are *strikingly ineffectual*.

Effectiveness stems from consciously consolidating blocks of discretionary time available during the week, then allocating one block of time for intentional, meaningful activities. For example, when you isolate 30 minutes a day for a specific purpose, you can combine the time into a 2 ½ hour block dedicated to valuable tasks like proactive relationship management.

In my coaching work and in managing my own time, I use two simple practices to make a significant difference in effectiveness. First, *own* your discretionary time, meaning the time you *control* on your calendar. Everyone must attend meetings someone else schedules – standing staff meetings, meetings with your manager, regulatory or other mandatory meetings. Most people control the remainder of their daily calendar time at work.

Second, *categorize* how you invest your time. Apply simple activity categorization to your calendar to draw your attention to areas you can improve. Make the categories relevant to you, but simple, like *Administrative Tasks*, *Relationship Time*, *New Ventures* (business development, new clients, new ideas, new projects), *Coaching Time* (either for you coaching or being coached), and *Lost Time* (time you cannot account for when reviewing your calendar).

To the extent possible, consolidate discretionary time into productivity blocks. Drucker emphasized the power of large blocks of uninterrupted time to do the things you do "uncommonly well;" time to do more of what you do best. In these intentionally allocated blocks of discretionary time, you can engage in Proactive Relationship Management.

Owning your calendar includes protecting your time. Be mindful of time wasters that creep into your life and rob you of productivity. Before you know it, these stealthy *incoming time bombs* blow up your calendar for the day. You can identify some easier than others. Distractions, such as incoming email, texts, instant messages, Tweets, Instagram notifications or other digital diversions soak up hours every day. People who drop by your workspace for a "quick question" are also distractions. It takes discipline to override a Pavlovian response to incoming time bombs, but the productivity boost is well worth the investment.

Creating a habit

Four Star General Colin Powell said, "If you're going to achieve excellence in big things, you develop the habit in little matters. Excellence is not an exception; it is a prevailing attitude."

You create time to invest in relationships for a *reason*. Professional relationships don't just happen; you intentionally cultivate them, develop them and nurture them. To build a foundation to lead from, create new habits: Identifying people you want to engage with, consciously develop relationships, and sustain them over time. *Leading from Where you Are* defines, designs and demonstrates how you show up in your work, how you make yourself valuable and influential to the organization, and how you garner support in your endeavors. Proactive Relationship Management, one *little matter* in the grand scheme, plays an oversized role in achieving excellence as a leader.

Paying it forward

Daniel Goleman anchored his seminal work in Emotional Intelligence (EQ) in five key elements - *Self-awareness, Self-regulation, Motivation, Empathy* and *Social Skills*. Our competence at demonstrating each of these elements affects our ability to notice our emotions and those of others, understand them, and manage them.

As we practice EQ in our professional relationships, we build trust, respect and equity with our colleagues. We earn the right to be in the relationship, and this investment creates mutual support with our colleagues. But be clear – we must invest first – pay it forward – in order to *earn the right* to be in the relationship.

Who do I engage?

While all professional relationships matter at some level, not all relationships are equally important. To help understand professional relationship relevance, imagine a set of three concentric circles, the smallest ring in the center, surrounded by a larger circle, both enfolded in a third, larger circle. Each circle represents a set of your professional relationships.

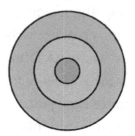

The center circle represents your closest relationships by virtue of the relevance of their role to your work. This group includes your direct manager, direct reports, and colleagues performing roles most important to your effectiveness and efficiency in performing your work. These will likely be the people you connect with daily or weekly. They are also the most mutually influential *now*. They influence you, you influence them, and together your ideas and actions impact each other's results. They are your *inner circle*.

The second circle includes people in roles relevant to the impact you make through your work, but to a lesser degree than your inner circle. This group includes colleagues in areas you work with less frequently – perhaps monthly or quarterly. Your work is important to this middle circle group, and vice-versa, but the tasks you perform together have lower-level urgency.

The outer circle represents people whose work may not have *direct and current* connection to yours today, but, have potential for relevance at some point.

When you determine which relationships in your professional sphere fall into each of the three circles, you can better prioritize the investment of dedicated time to Proactive Relationship Management. Once you block time on your calendar, identify with whom and how you want to invest that time each week, then initiate meaningful outreach with the intention to develop or expand relationships.

I've practiced this approach for years with impactful results. I found that some of the people I developed relationships with began in the outer circle but ended up moving to my inner circle. Someone got a promotion, a job transfer, or the company reorganized. Suddenly people in roles most relevant to my effectiveness changed. My proactive relationship management investments paid nice dividends over time, like being assigned to a new boss who I already knew.

What do I say?

Pete had a gruff nature. Over the phone he sounded like Tony Soprano's taciturn twin brother. We both worked for the same bank – Pete in Chicago, me in Los Angeles. He worked for a company recently acquired by my bank. Integration of the two companies was still a work-in-progress. Our paths were about to cross, but until then we had never met each other.

The company launched a new project to evaluate effectiveness of operations across the enterprise as merger integration neared completion. My boss asked me to lead the project for my division and gave me the names of some subject matter experts to help with the endeavor. Pete was one of them. I was excited to kick things off so as a first step, I called Pete to introduce myself and talk about a project we'd be working on together.

At first, I thought I dialed the wrong number. The voice on the other end of the phone line simply croaked "Yeah."

I said, "Is this Pete?"

"Yeah."

No "Hello, this is Pete" or "This is Pete at Standard Bank" like I expected.

The call didn't get much better. I tried to engage Pete but couldn't get far. "I understand we're going to be working on a project together for a while."

I heard a sharp, "Yeah."

I said, "I understand you're a master at this type of analysis."

"Uh huh."

I wondered what I was doing wrong. Maybe Pete's unhappy about the merger, or, didn't want to work together. I felt frustrated with the lack of connection, and closed the call with, "There's an in-person meeting scheduled in San Francisco later in the month. I hope you'll be there."

All he said was, "I will."

I wasn't sure what to expect when the new make-shift project team came together for our first in-person meeting, but I knew that Pete would be an important part of the group dynamic and ultimately, our success (or lack thereof).

He was the only member of the team I hadn't previously met, so I arranged for us to visit 30 minutes before our group meeting.

We met in front of the bank building, then walked half a block to a coffee shop. As we strolled down the street, we passed a hole-in-the-wall pizza restaurant.

I said, "There's a lot of good food in San Francisco, but so far, they haven't cracked the code for good pizza."

Pete stopped walking. I thought I'd offended him.

He turned to me, made direct eye contact for the first time, and said with the authority of a Michelin-star restaurant judge, "I totally agree. There's no pizza like *New York* pizza."

I said, "Aren't you from Chicago? Don't you feel some sense of hometown loyalty to deep dish pies?"

"I'm originally from New York," Pete said. "I moved to Chicago to go to college, but never accepted Chicago-style pizza as the real thing. They used too much dough and not enough flavor."

We spent the entire time that morning talking about one of our favorite shared interests – pizza! My first impression was wrong. Pete turned out to be a warm, engaging person once we found a topic of common interest to talk about. Over time, we talked about a lot of things – family, hobbies, travel, movies, and our project at the bank. We developed a valuable relationship that rewarded us both on multiple levels. From that experience, I learned that the specifics of how to create an opportunity to engage with someone are less important than *making the effort to engage.* Pizza wasn't the reason our paths intersected, but it turned out to be a wonderful topic to develop our relationship.

It might feel uncomfortable to initiate a conversation with someone you don't know. Nobody wants to annoy another person or be intrusive. It's easy to feel we're invading someone's privacy if we connect out of context (meaning without a specific task to complete).

This normal perception is likely rooted in a false belief that the other person isn't interested in knowing you better. The good news: As co-workers, you already have a common frame of reference to begin a new conversation – your company.

Mastering the Art of Inquiry chapter goes into detail about how to approach conversations for learning about colleagues. The take-away is to always be prepared for expected (planned) and unexpected opportunities for relationship development.

For *planned conversations* to get to know a coworker better, deliberately write out three to five discussion-framing questions and memorize them to prepare for a dialog. When you meet the co-worker, you can blend your prepared questions into a natural conversation.

For best results, keep your *go-to questions* tucked away in the back of your mind. Simple questions like "what was it about our company that made you decide to work here?", "what did you do before you came into your current role?", or "how do you feel your work aligns with what you do best?" are great conversation starters. When you prepare in advance, you'll be more comfortable with the conversation's flow, and you'll be in position to get to know a colleague – an essential first step in developing a more meaningful relationship.

Building trust

Trust, the foundation of every relationship, takes time to develop and can disappear in a flash. Build it through communication, observation and experience, demonstrate that your words are true, and do what you say you'll do.

Trust comes when you do what you say you'll do, own your mistakes, make decisions and take actions that serve a greater good, not simply your self-interest.

Another often overlooked aspect of trust is the *realness factor* - our confidence in displaying authenticity, vulnerability and candor. Realness is not about telling people what we believe they want to hear.

Hans Christian Andersen's fable of the *Emperor's New Clothes* is a good illustration. In this story, two unscrupulous tailors called on the Emperor to sell him a special new suit. The tailors convinced the Emperor that the new suit they proposed to craft for him was invisible.

The Emperor loved buying new clothes and always wanted the latest styles and finest fabrics for his outfits. He thought a new suit woven from invisible cloth would be the perfect addition to his wardrobe. Off went the tailors with the suit order in hand to begin creating the Emperor's new suit.

When the tailors returned the following week to deliver the special new invisible suit, the Emperor asked one of his trusted cabinet ministers to be the first to see him wear the new garment. Unfortunately, when the Emperor modeled the suit, the cabinet minister thought to himself – oh no, I don't see anything at all! But he was afraid to tell the Emperor, who was excited about his special new invisible suit. After showing the cabinet minister the new suit, the Emperor decided to parade before his subjects in his new suit so they too could share his excitement. Not a single subject dared say they didn't see the new suit on him for fear of appearing stupid. Finally, a child cried out, "The Emperor isn't wearing anything at all!" The moral of this story is a threefold message:

- Realness is critical to developing and sustaining trust
- Realness comes from having the confidence to demonstrate *candor* (honest, sincere forthrightness), *authenticity* (true to one's self) and *vulnerability* (willingness to risk expressing one's view)
- The absence of realness increases the risk of damage to a relationship.

To intentionally develop and sustain trust is the heart of Proactive Relationship Management. You might feel uncomfortable when you intentionally initiate conversations and relationship development activities with someone you don't know very well, but the benefits far outweigh the effort to overcome initial inertia.

Steps to practice in Proactive Relationship Management

1. Intentionally block time on your calendar for Proactive Relationship Management time every week.
2. Identify the people in roles with the greatest relevance to your work and prioritize who you will engage and how often.
3. Be prepared with mindful conversation starters and conversation topics.
4. Recognize the importance of building and sustaining trust in relationships.

5. Understand how to practice realness in your relationships.

Chapter 2
Mastering the Art of Inquiry

I'm convinced the old adage "curiosity killed the cat" was coined by a cat hater and has nothing to do with curiosity! In reality, curiosity *fuels* creativity, creativity *animates* innovation and innovation helps organizations reinvent themselves to sustain relevance. The Art of Inquiry (asking meaningful questions) makes curiosity come to life.

Recently, Sara, one of my daughter's friends, dog sat for a couple who live in Manhattan while they vacationed. The subject of the assignment: Rusty, a good-natured Golden Retriever in his twilight years. Over the previous few months of his seventeenth year, Rusty began to experience health issues. His owners were concerned about being so far from home given Rusty's condition, but they'd planned their vacation for more than a year and felt comfortable with Sara staying in their apartment, on duty with Rusty, while they toured Europe.

On Saturday, the third day of her dog sitting assignment, when she woke in the morning, Sara glanced over at Rusty laying in his dog bed.

Sara got out of bed and noticed Rusty didn't react to the sound of her bare feet stepping onto the hardwood floor.

"Good morning Rusty."

No reaction.

"*Rusty*?" Still, nothing.

She inched toward the dog's bed, turning on the bedroom light en route. When she got close enough, she nudged Rusty's bed with her big toe. Nothing. One more shove, this time with her full foot. No response.

Sara bent over, focused closely to look for signs of life, but saw overwhelming evidence to the contrary. Rusty's time on this earth had expired. Sara wanted to reach out and pet Rusty but the idea of touching a dead dog kept her from acting. She felt horrible; sad about Rusty's passing and guilty that he passed away under her watch.

After a few minutes of processing her own grief, she called Rusty's owners to share the news. While the call was difficult to make, the owners were not completely surprised Rusty passed.

After the initial emotion of the conversation, the owners asked, "Sara, can you take Rusty to his veterinarian? The vet knows what to do and will take care of all necessary details."

Without thinking through the logistics of getting Rusty's body to the vet, Sara said, "Okay."

Like a lot of New Yorkers, Sara didn't own a car, which made getting Rusty to the vet for his proper disposition more complex. She considered different ideas, like calling the humane society, taking Rusty in an Uber, and a few other options. Then she thought up her best idea to transport the dead Golden Retriever: Place him in the oversized roller suitcase she used to carry her clothes to the dog sitting assignment.

First, Sara needed to maneuver the dog fully inside the suitcase, no small feat since Golden Retrievers are large dogs. Once she secured him and closed the latches, she needed to get the roller suitcase to the subway station and on a train for the commute to the veterinarian's office. The last step: deliver Rusty to the vet for transition to his final resting place.

With Rusty packed in, Sara rolled the bulky, oversized suitcase out to the elevator, down to the building lobby, and out to the street. From there, she traversed four blocks to the subway station.

Sara boarded her train and found a seat near the end of an aisle to position herself for an easy exit when she and Rusty arrived at their subway stop. She sat with one hand lightly gripping the suitcase handle to keep it steady during the ride.

Halfway to their destination, the train made one of its regular stops. While passengers got on and off the train, Sara felt the handle on the suitcase slide out of her hand and away from her. By the time she processed what happened, she realized a thief grabbed the roller suitcase handle, yanked it away, and ran out of the train as the subway doors closed. She watched in shock through the subway window as the thief ran through the crowd pulling her suitcase behind him. The unsuspecting perpetrator had grabbed *something he thought he wanted* but had no idea what he actually got!

Have you ever gotten something you *thought* you wanted, only to be surprised when you found out it wasn't what you expected?

The value of curiosity cannot be overstated. Practicing curiosity helps us grow and tune in to opportunities that can be meaningful in our work and life. Curiosity comes to life through asking meaningful questions, learning, expanding our perspectives and gaining clarity about what we want before we reach for something.

Brian Grazer has produced some of the most well-known television shows and movies of the past four decades. Along with his partner, Ron Howard, Brian co-founded Imagine Entertainment, which produced dozens of highly successful shows including *24*, *Parenthood*, *Lie to Me*, and *Empire*. Grazer's movie catalogue includes classics like *A Beautiful Mind*, *The Da Vinci Code*, and *Apollo 13*. In addition to financial success, movies and television shows have earned Brian nominations for 43 Academy Awards and 195 Emmy Awards. In 2007, Grazer was named one of *Time* magazine's most influential people in the world.

Brian built his career through the art of inquiry driven by curiosity. He said, "Curiosity is what gives energy and insight to everything else I do. I love show business. I love telling stories. But I loved being curious long before I loved the movie business. For me, curiosity infuses everything with a sense of possibility. Curiosity has, quite literally, been the key to my success, and the key to my happiness."

In *A Curious Mind: The Secret to a Bigger Life*, Grazer said, "The secret that we don't seem to understand, the wonderful connection we're not making: Curiosity is the tool that sparks creativity. Curiosity is the technique that gets to innovation. Questions create a mind-set of innovation and creativity. Curiosity presumes that there might be something new out there. Curiosity presumes that there might be something outside our own experience out there. Curiosity allows the possibility that the way we're doing it now isn't the only way, or even the best way."

Curiosity is at the heart of Mastering the Art of Inquiry. Merriam-Webster defines *art* as a skill acquired by experience, study, or observation. Developing this skill comes from building and demonstrating comfort in asking meaningful, probing questions, letting responses guide subsequent questions in order to understand a topic, and doing so in a natural, conversational manner. Mastering the Art of Inquiry allows you learn more about the ideas, interests and concerns of your colleagues, customers, competitors and vendors.

Why is Mastering the Art of Inquiry so important as a leadership practice? Warren Berger, author of *A More Beautiful Question: The Power of Inquiry to Spark Breakthrough Ideas*, presents a three-part problem-solving framework built upon *why, what if* and *how to* questions. Berger builds a compelling case for practicing the art of inquiry through an open, curious mind to fuel new possibilities, generate creative ideas, and achieve better outcomes. In research on how inventors, designers and engineers develop ideas and solve problems, Berger found that "brilliant changemakers" shared a common trait: They were exceptionally good at asking questions.

Asking good questions helps discover what matters, where opportunities exist, and how to find them. The National Question Week website (yes, there is a national question week in the U.S. each March) says that, "Questioning is a critical tool for learning. It helps us solve problems and adapt to change. And increasingly, we're coming to understand that it is a starting point for innovation.

"In a world of dynamic change, one could say that questions are becoming more important than answers. Today, what we "know" may quickly become outdated or obsolete—and we must constantly question to get to new and better answers.

"Questions also spark the imagination. And we're now learning that questions can help us motivate ourselves much better than resolutions or statements—all the while engaging the interest and support of others. Learning how to act on our inquiry can lead us toward solutions and creative breakthroughs. Einstein understood this; as do the people running Google, Amazon, and lots of other innovative endeavors."

Curiosity leads to questions, which is how we bring the Art of Inquiry to life. Meaningful questions are incredibly powerful for guiding discovery and learning. Successful leaders know they don't have all the answers, so the value of their contribution emanates from asking great questions.

In a recent Harvard Business Review article, authors Alison Wood Brooks and Leslie K. John discussed the power of questions as tools for unlocking value in an organization to stimulate learning and exchange ideas.

These authors posit that building our skills in asking meaningful questions, which can fuel innovation and better performance, builds trust among team members and can also help mitigate risk by uncovering unforeseen issues an organization faces. Unfortunately, according to Wood Brooks and John, "Most of us don't ask enough questions, nor do we pose our inquiries in an optimal way. The good news is that by asking questions, we naturally improve our emotional intelligence, which in turn makes us better questioners - a virtuous cycle."

So why not refer to this leadership practice as mastering the art of questioning? *Inquiry* is more than asking good questions.

It is *the purposeful act of seeking knowledge through questions*. Mastering the Art of Inquiry means building a competency that facilitates the exchange of knowledge and contributes to the development of relationships, where both knowledge exchange and relationship development are equally important. Think of Mastering the Art of Inquiry as a leadership practice that invites inclusion and engagement among colleagues and stakeholders.

Some of us are curious by nature. We possess an innate desire to learn through inquiry. Others may need to consciously develop competency in the art of inquiry.

Whether natural or a developmental opportunity, mastering this competency is essential in *Leading from Where you Are*. In every organization, the company needs to know more about team members, customers, competition, the offering, and more and more.

Formal research is one dimension of sourcing new information. This *Leading from Where you Are* theme is based on your role as a contributor to your organization's learning prowess.

Curiosity and good questions

There's no such thing as a bad question, but there is a matter of relevance. The more purposeful a question, the more likely it is relevant. As you practice the Art of Inquiry and express authentic curiosity with purpose, your business environment can guide questions. A helpful framework to inform relevant questions is to apply a deductive view of a situation, whether it is a team meeting, project discussion, or a conversation with a colleague. I like the metaphor of a funnel to represent deductive thinking and how to develop an understanding of context. The top of a funnel – the widest part – represents the bigger picture of a situation; the bottom end reflects specific details. If you are working on a project that impacts several parts of your organization, some of the bigger picture contextual questions may include:

1. What is the purpose of the project?
2. How did it come about?
3. What does success look like?
4. How does this endeavor fit into the broader organizational mission?
5. Why was company leadership willing to commit to this project?
6. What if the organization would not have undertaken this endeavor?
7. How does this project leverage our competencies as an organization?
8. What are some of the risks we need to be cognizant of with this endeavor?
9. Who else in the company should we be speaking with to gather their insights on this work?
10. Have other organizations taken on similar projects, and if so, what can we learn from their experience?
11. Who are the subject matter experts in this area and how can we access them?

These bigger picture contextual questions can help in developing a deeper understanding and create fodder to frame more specific tactical questions of relevance to the project.

The why behind the why

Through practicing the Art of Inquiry, creating clarity about *what* you want to know begins with *why*, and why speaks to purpose. Good questions support the purpose of expanding knowledge which serves to enhance your contribution to the mission of the organization. The *why* behind good questions is always anchored in beneficial learning.

In contrast, questions should not be used to further a personal agenda or feed ego; inauthenticity is easy to spot and discredits the questioner.

Charles was a regional manager with CEO aspirations. He had early career success as an individual contributor, which catapulted him into management roles at an early age. His quick rise and reputation as a high-potential leader gave Charles a spotlight most managers with his tenure didn't have. Charles worked hard to make certain his team delivered the results he expected and put the same level of energy into making sure his superiors knew how hard he worked.

Charles reported to a senior executive with the company who not only served as a supportive manager, but also as a mentor and advocate for him. She saw great potential in Charles and didn't let his overtly ambitious demeanor interfere with her perceptions of his capabilities. Less than a year into his regional manager role, Charles' boss announced she was leaving the company to take a position with a competitor. Along with the departure news was an announcement of the replacement manager for the senior executive role.

The new executive was introduced to Charles and his peers, a group of about forty managers, on a conference call shortly after the announcement was made. The new manager talked about his background with the company, the excitement he had about his new assignment and the approach he planned to take to business growth. After the introductory comments, participants were invited to ask questions of the new executive.

Charles was the first person to speak up. He prefaced his question by saying, "Welcome to the group. We're glad to have you join us, and to help you get to know the team better, let me take a minute before I ask my question to tell you about my background with the company."

Charles described his role, then mentioned the work his team did to develop new business opportunities, how aggressively he took on competitors in the market and the results he expected to produce by year-end. By the time Charles got to his question, he discounted the relevance of anything he could ask the new executive.

Rather than asking a meaningful question to learn more about the new leader and his plans, Charles used the conference call to further his personal agenda of moving further up in the company. Charles missed an opportunity to learn about his new boss and his priorities and fueled a perception that he was not authentic or interested in anything other than himself. The executive handled Charles' grandstanding diplomatically on the call by saying, "Thanks for the background information Charles; now that we've met, I won't need to visit your region until I get to know people in all the other markets." Coincidentally, Charles was transferred to a different position in another division soon after the new executive's arrival.

The value of questioning the way we've always done things

A well-known disclosure in the investment business is: *Past performance is no guarantee of future results.* The statement means that all the conditions in the past – the economy, capital markets, employment, consumer spending, capital investments, and the nature of specific investments – created an outcome that may not necessarily be repeated in the future as conditions change. In a sense, this statement is prophetic. It tells us that we can't *rely* on our history to define the future. Yet in business, inquiry can help us determine what to preserve and what to disrupt.

One Saturday afternoon, a young boy watched his parents prepare dinner in the kitchen. He closely watched his mom cut off both ends of a pot roast, then throw the ends into the garbage before she put the meat in a pan to cook for dinner.

The boy was curious about the process and asked, "Why do you cut off the ends of the roast and throw them away?"

His mom paused for a moment then said, "I'm not sure why I cut the ends off, but I learned to cook from my mom, and that's the way she always prepared a roast."

The next time the boy's grandmother came for a visit, his mother asked, "Mom, why do you always cut the ends off of a pot roast before cooking it?"

Her mother said, "Well, when I first moved out on my own as a young woman, I lived in a small apartment with a very small kitchen and a tiny oven. I bought a small roast pan that fit the oven just right. In order to make the roast fit the pan, I had to cut the ends off."

The moral of this story is that it's important to understand *why* things are done in a certain way. Asking good questions is a powerful technique to develop understanding so you can determine how to challenge answers that may not make sense in the current environment.

We hear that nothing great is ever achieved by doing things the way they've always been done. It's hard to imagine that today any organization or industry is mired in a legacy approach to anything. I often assume that the dynamic nature of operating environments, technology, consumers and regulations keeps everything open for refinement in business. As the pot roast story illustrates, that's not the case.

I once led a project team tasked with streamlining the process for opening new investment accounts, which were subject to regulatory scrutiny to make sure the investor was not laundering money or financing terrorist activities. To meet government and company requirements, investors were required to complete multiple documents. Some of the forms didn't make sense to investors.

One form seemed unnecessary based on then current regulatory requirements. I asked our compliance officer, "Do you know why new clients need to complete this form?"

She said, "I don't know, but it's not a compliance department requirement. Why don't you ask the legal department to see if they have the answer?"

Next, I visited the attorney helping our team to ask the same question. Her response sounded strikingly familiar to the compliance answer. "I don't know, but it's not a legal department requirement. Why don't you ask the operations department to see if they have the answer?"

I asked colleagues in operations, risk management, marketing and sales. Nobody "owned" that annoying form. I finally learned that about twenty years earlier, an old policy required the form in question. The company discontinued that policy five years later. Over the next decade, the company made every new investment client fill out this unnecessary document, adding more time to a process we were trying to streamline.

How do we challenge long-lived ideas or processes respectfully and authentically? Challenging for its own sake can come off as self-serving and disrespectful. The approach recommended here is to ask meaningful, well-thought-out questions with a purpose and remaining open-minded to the answers.

Empathy, understanding another's perspective, is equally important in Mastering the Art of Inquiry. Standard operating procedures were developed for *some* reason. Perhaps the initial reason for an approach is outdated, but at some point in time, the reason made sense to the people who put it in place. Embedding empathy in your approach to inquiry helps build understanding and better informs you how to approach new questions about existing procedures.

Steps to practice in Mastering the Art of Inquiry

1. Recognize how authentic curiosity and Mastering the Art of Inquiry create the pathway to develop understanding, build meaningful relationships and expand knowledge.
2. Build a repertoire of open-ended purposeful questions to guide conversations.
3. Frame questions around points of curiosity that will contribute to a meaningful conversation.
4. Listen for invitations for follow-on questions.
5. Develop confidence in diplomatically asking *why* questions.

Chapter 3
Nurturing Ideation

"My favorite thing about teaching fourth graders is seeing the lightbulbs come on when they get a new idea."

When Chris, a fourth-grade teacher, spoke these words during my son's back to school night, I imagined every parent in the room saw a cartoon lightbulb switch on above their child's head to announce the birth of another brilliant new idea. The notion that an idea emerges fully developed captivates us so much that a fourth-grade classroom filled with parents or a boardroom filled with senior executives embraces it with open arms. Ironic symbolism.

Felix the Cat, one of the first animated cartoon stars, made his debut in 1919 in the silent era of film. Since he couldn't speak, Felix's animators used symbols and text boxes above his head to express what the mischievous, fun-loving feline wanted to communicate. Felix became popular with a wide audience excited to go to the theater to see what antics he would perform in each episode.

In a 1924 episode, fans watched a lightbulb pop up above Felix's head when an idea about how to rescue a golfer's lost ball emerged. Over time, the notion of a lightbulb over someone's head became symbolic of giving immediate birth to a new idea.

The irony is in the symbol itself. The idea behind the incandescent lightbulb didn't grow from a single flash of brilliance. Many scientists worked to develop incandescent lighting devices beginning in the early 1800s, when an Italian inventor, Alessandro Volta, developed a glowing copper wire, one of the first manifestations of incandescent lighting. Over the next eighty years, inventors and scientists in Europe, Canada and the United States built a library of lightbulb development concepts.

Later in the century, Thomas Edison and his research team in Menlo Park, New Jersey entered the picture. They built momentum after years of research, testing more than three thousand light bulb designs between 1878 and 1880. Edison filed his patent for a carbon filament electric lamp in 1879. Flash of genius? No. Nurturing Ideation? Absolutely!

Nurturing Ideation is *the intentional process of feeding growth and development of ideas with the goal of application.* We tend to think of breakthroughs in science, technology or business as *events*. We hear about a new development that will make our lives simpler or better in some way, and think it resulted from *one brilliant idea.* In real world, breakthroughs emerge from an accumulation of ideas nurtured through a series of iterations over time.

Consider the idea of industry disruption. Points of evolution lead to a paradigm shift, which changes the way a certain process is done. Iteration builds, then crescendos into a new product or process which looks different. In isolation, the new methods appear to be revolutionary; in context they're the result of evolution.

The World Economic Forum describes the Fourth Industrial Revolution as *a fusion of technologies blurring the lines between the physical, digital, and biological spheres*[2]. Sounds revolutionary, right? When you add the context of the First Industrial Revolution, which used water and steam power to mechanize production, the Second, which used electric power to create mass production, and the Third, which used electronics and information technology to automate production, it becomes clear the Fourth Industrial Revolution emerged from an *evolution* of applied ideas; Nurturing Ideation on a macro scale.

Today, we access dozens of information and entertainment platforms which evolved from an idea developed in the last century and continue to add new applications today. Radio technology presented the world with the first-ever platform for real-time mass communication because a series of ideas fueled an accretive development that began in the mid 1800's.

In 1860, an American dentist, Mahlon Loomis, experimented with electricity applications. After eight years of development, Loomis demonstrated *wireless telegraphy*, a communication system which enabled him to send an electric signal over 14 miles using kites connected to copper wire.

In 1886, a German physicist, Heinrich Hertz, took the idea further when he demonstrated that he could transmit radio waves wirelessly. Nikola Tesla further nurtured the work of Loomis and Hertz when he developed and demonstrated a wireless radio to audiences in St. Louis in 1893.

The following year, Guglielmo Marconi, an Italian inventor, demonstrated the ability to send a wireless transmission over 30 feet. In 1901, he transmitted the first signal across the

---

[2] https://www.weforum.org/agenda/2016/01/the-fourth-industrial-revolution-what-it-means-and-how-to-respond/

Atlantic, from Europe to North America. Shortly after that, through additional ideations, in 1906 the first Amplitude Modulation (AM) radio transmission took place from a garage in Brant Rock, Massachusetts.

Each of these ideas expanded on existing inventions in telegraph and the telephone technology, feeding satellite radio, cell phone and Wi-Fi development, reflecting ideation across different countries and people who didn't intentionally collaborate in nurturing ideation. The stories become more engaging when they take place within a single firm focused on development and innovation.

Koen Frenken, an innovation scientist at Utrecht University in the Netherlands, researches the origins of revolutionary innovations, concentrating on whether people with non-standard backgrounds are more likely to create scientific, technological and cultural breakthroughs.

Frenken compares the mixture of ideation inspirations to a *family tree,* an amalgamation of the *pedigrees* of various ideas, where knowledge, instead of DNA, is transmitted across branches. The more varied the ideas which combine into something new, the higher the potential for radical innovation.

Frenken believes his concept of *ideas-evolution* applies in music, art, business and science. The richness of idea evolution comes from the breadth of ideators contributing to the process. In Frenken's view, by drawing from people with varied backgrounds, perspectives and experiences, organizations can build a bastion of knowledge that enables them to see links where others can't.

Putting ideation into action is the lifeblood of any organization, the genesis and sustenance that allows an organization to survive. Every institution, nonprofit enterprise, small, medium, large or global business on the planet today, or at any time in history, began with a single idea which it nurtured and developed. *Sustainable ideation* is the fundamental fuel source that allows an organization to continue and grow.

Nurturing Ideation speaks to initiating new, actionable ideas for your organization, supporting and encouraging others to do the same, and constructively riffing-off ideas brought into conversation for exploration. It doesn't mean indiscriminate support for every idea presented; that's disingenuous.

Understanding the value of ideas

Organizations need new ideas to serve their stakeholders. Successful organizations continually enhance their offerings to sustain relevance. Individual contributors with an understanding of processes, interactions with customers, vendors and partners are often in the right place to source and evolve new, actionable ideas.

A common practice in Japanese organizations is known as Kaizen, or "good change." Roots of this philosophy are partially credited to management consultant and professor W. Edwards Deming, best known for his work in the area of continuous improvement and quality control in manufacturing. In his book, *Out of the Crisis*, Deming outlines his key principles for transforming business effectiveness. He believed that businesses must improve their system of production and service constantly forever. He said transformation is everybody's job. In Deming's view, people from different disciplines in a company need to break down barriers and work as a team to foresee production problems they may encounter with the product or service. At the roots of good change are new ideas that contribute to continuous improvement.

The source of great ideas

Some organizations have dedicated research and development teams or innovation labs which are integral to ongoing growth. Those areas generally represent a different aspect of ideation. The challenge companies often face is how they access and operationalize new ideas from outside the company. Great ideas come from multiple sources and *Leading from Where you Are* means *seeing yourself as an active contributor to ideation through inquiry, initiating and iterating.* The call to action: Build your acumen in developing, packaging and presenting new and evolving ideas as part of the value you add to your organization.

Here are three specific actions you can take to build your contribution to ideation:

1. Practice summarizing a new idea in its simplest form. Einstein said *if you can't explain something simply, you don't understand it.* Or, in the words of a wonderful manager from early in my career, "When you bring a new idea to me, pretend you're explaining it to your 90-year-old grandfather; if you get him to understand the idea, I'll understand it too." Earl was a great teacher. His message rings true across all aspects of sharing new ideas. The more you practice distilling new ideas into their simplest form, the more comfortable the process becomes. People can always ask you for more detail if they need it.

2. Identify the areas of greatest need in your organization. Ideas for their own sake are fun. Ideas that can be

applied are meaningful. Ideas that address an issue or open-up new opportunities for your company are *valuable*. You have your areas of subject matter expertise and hold a level of organizational knowledge that extends beyond your specific niche; opportunity identification is a blend of both. Good questions to ask yourself about the potential benefit of new ideas include:

- "What are the biggest challenges being discussed in the company right now?"
- "Where are new opportunities to expand our business by improving some aspect of our offering?"
- "What the process challenges do I see the most often?"
- "When I first came into my job, what were the practices/activities that didn't make sense to me?"

The point of these questions is to focus your attention on needs within the company that can benefit from your knowledge, experience and curiosity.

3. Practice non-attachment to the outcome when you offer an idea. Non-attachment is not indifference, which means apathy and disinterest. Non-attachment refers to our ability to present an idea with clear intention of contributing to the organization, *and* being comfortable with the outcome, even if our idea it is not embraced. It's easy to react and feel rejected. Taking the risk of presenting something new means being vulnerable and open, even if the outcome isn't what we hoped.

How to meaningfully add to ideas of others

I started playing guitar when I was fourteen. The first six months of lessons covered chords and fundamentals of music. The first few months of learning this instrument are the hardest part physically. The fingertips on my left hand hurt as I developed callouses from pressing on the guitar strings. I experienced muscle pain in my hands and forearms as I built stamina holding down chords.

For me, the pain was well worth the gain. I soon developed a level of comfort with the fundamentals that prepared me to venture into experimenting with playing solos. After working on my regular lesson, I would put on an album of one of my favorite bands, figure out what key a song was in, then start hitting single notes that sounded like the song's melody. Copying melody lines led to my own improvising by playing patterns that didn't already exist in the song. I learned to add riffs to existing solos and at various places throughout the song. It was great fun, but also required discipline since it's very easy to overplay and add riffs where they don't belong because it's so much fun.

Outside of the music realm, *stream of consciousness thinking* is also referred to as riffing. In terms of *Leading from Where you Are*, riffing means *to meaningfully add to an idea developed by someone else*. As with music, ideation riffing requires discipline and being mindful not to "overplay".

Imagine you're working on a project with a colleague who is evaluating new inventory management software packages for use in your company's distribution center. Her diligence narrowed alternatives to a single recommendation, and she's now developing plans for transition to the new software. She suggests doing the transition at the end of a month so the company can capitalize on implementation after it closes the books for the period. Because other work you do intersects with the distribution center, you know that deliveries of new product received over the next 90 days will include the addition of many new SKUs. You believe that a month-end transition over the next quarter will introduce a number of new variables which add to the complexity of transitioning to the new inventory system, so you add to your co-worker's month-end idea with a suggestion to schedule the move over a holiday weekend the following quarter. The three-day weekend allows more time before business-as-usual resumes the Tuesday after the holiday. You've added to your colleague's idea in a manner that increases opportunities for a successful transition and reduces risks associated with the system change.

The way you present ingredients you'd like to offer to build on an existing idea matters. As with riffing in music, tuning into to the right place and time for an addition can make the difference between beautiful music with a natural flow and a cacophony.

Steps toward a positive impact through Nurturing Ideation:

Read the idea initiator. Is she open to expanding her idea or more closed? Does the idea appear to be a foregone conclusion in its current state or is it still in the formation stage? Is this an original idea, or one that's been passed along from another source for implementation?

Read the environment – Is the situation addressed with this idea part of the business-as-usual environment, or more urgent? Is the idea driven from within your organization (self-initiated) or from outside (by customers, regulation, competitors)?

Understand the context – Is this idea a stand-alone situation or part of a broader action in your company? How does this idea align with other strategic contingencies or considerations?

Delving into these questions to inform your approach prepares you to optimize your contribution to ideation. As with riffing in music, the better feel you have for the timing and flow of ideation, the more your actions can add to the outcome.

Steps to practice in Nurturing Ideation

1. Recognize the iterative nature of ideation and consider how your individual competencies can serve as ingredients that add to the process.
2. Identify those organization-wide activities your work is closest to and be clear about how your work fits into the broader ecosystem of the company. From that vantage point, look at each touchpoint for improvement iterations and use this as inspiration for ideation.
3. Practice reading your environment for opportunities to offer new ideas or meaningfully add to the ideas of others. As with riffing in music, knowing when to float an idea can be as important as the idea itself.
4. Apply lessons from Mastering the Art of Inquiry to source invitations to contribute to ideation.
5. Demonstrate enthusiasm for the ideas you present while practicing non-attachment to the outcome.

Chapter 4
Merchandising Knowledge

Knowledge is power! You've heard or perhaps made that statement, which asserts that the more knowledge a person develops, the smarter they are, and ipso facto, the more powerful they are.

This idea goes back many centuries. Some attribute its origin to English philosopher Sir Francis Bacon, who wrote "ipsa scientia potestas est" or "knowledge itself is power."

Is knowledge *really* power? Maybe not.

A modern fable tells the story of a brilliant software developer who designed apps that changed people's lives with little effort on the part of the user. One day, he showed his former college roommate a new prototype app the developer wanted to share with the world. He explained to his friend how the app worked, the problem it solved, and how easily it integrated into a user's daily life. The app impressed his friend.

The developer showed his new app to a couple of software engineers he knew from graduate school. They were so impressed they asked to look at the source code, which they read with great excitement.

The developer decided to seek funding to produce his new product. He got an appointment to show his app and a pitch deck he created to one of the preeminent venture capital firms, located on Sand Hill Road in the heart of Silicon Valley.

He arrived filled with confidence. In the meeting, he walked a group of investors through the underlying logic and technical structure of his app. He described the source code in precise detail, showing that he had extraordinary knowledge about his field.

Then, just as he thought his pitch reached a crescendo, the lead VC partner at the presentation said, *"We've seen enough...thanks for stopping by today. We'll be in touch."*

The software developer left the meeting, never heard from the VC people again.

If knowledge was power, the software engineer's presentation should have been incredibly potent. The venture capital people should have been awestruck with his brilliance and committed to invest in his new app.

That's not the way it worked out. In real life, brilliant people often miss the mark in Merchandising Knowledge. The *real* power of knowledge stems from distilling it into its simplest components, then making it applicable and actionable.

Jerry Weissman, a corporate presentation coach with years of experience, helps clients convert their knowledge into compelling messages. Weissman worked with executives from some of the world's largest companies including Intel, Intuit, Cisco, Microsoft, and Netflix, as well as private enterprises around the world.

He believes most business presentations serve to convey data, not to persuade. In his book *Presenting to Win*, Weissman says, "The person who is able to tell an effective story is perceived as being in command and deserves the confidence of others."

He describes five cardinal sins in presenting - no clear point, no audience benefit, no clear flow, too detailed and too long. Weissman describes one common denominator that includes all these presentation sins – the *data dump,* an excessive, meaningless, shapeless outpouring of data without purpose. Audiences react to the data dump not with persuasion, but with a "dreadful effect known as MEGO – Mine Eyes Glaze Over."

Weissman doesn't say that the more *knowledge* you present, the more powerful you are. His message is the opposite.

Traditionally, *merchandising* refers to promoting the sale of goods or products in a retail channel. In *Leading from Where you Are*, Merchandising Knowledge refers to *the act of sharing and promoting knowledge, distilled to its' simplest message, in an actionable form.* Key characteristics of this definition are to *simplify* knowledge, make it *actionable*, and *promote* it to those who can benefit from applying the knowledge.

Distilling knowledge into simple messages can be challenging. Simplification requires developing a deep understanding of the knowledge area within which you operate.

If the software developer applied this principle in the fable that opened this chapter, he might get a different outcome. In the revised story, the software engineer practiced the principle of Merchandising Knowledge and distilled the story supporting his new app to a single sentence: *"Using this app will help busy professionals save up to 30 minutes each day – two and a half hours every week – just by enhancing their time management effectiveness."*

This meets the definition of the principle as it promotes knowledge distilled to its' simplest message (using this app saves time) in an actionable form (enhance your time management effectiveness).

P.T. Barnum, founder of the Barnum & Bailey circus, once said, "Always leave them wanting more." This means to give your audience just enough to satisfy them and whet their appetite, so they come back for another visit.

Applied to Merchandising Knowledge, you present a headline describing the knowledge you want to share and let your audience, a single individual or a group, ask for more details. This approach stimulates interest in your topic, invites your audience to react to your thesis statement, then provides them an opportunity to tell you where they'd like more information. It also minimizes the risk of MEGO while increasing the potential for your audience to engage with the knowledge you share. That is power!

Making knowledge simple

Less is more when it comes to the practice of distilling and sharing knowledge. How do you simplify?

In their book *Simple: Conquering the Crisis of Complexity*, authors Alan Siegel and Irene Etzkorn describe an epidemic they believe is wreaking havoc on business, government and finance. Siegel and Etzkorn say people mistakenly believe more information equals greater clarity. Too much information overwhelms, creates fuzziness, and ultimately places people in an environment where they are apt to lose sight of what's important and stop paying attention. This is the crises of complexity. What's the solution? Siegel and Etzkorn describe three elements of simplification:

Empathize – Imagine the context in which someone will buy, read, or use the product or service you're offering, then create a design which reflects those needs. Empathizing emphasizes understanding another's thought processes, decision-making strategies and attention spans.

Distill – Boil down an offering to its essence. Curate, edit, and lessen the options and choices that can overwhelm.

Clarify – make an offering, service or product easier to understand, use and benefit from.

For *Leading from Where you Are*, we adapt the *Simple* steps to making knowledge simple:

Understand who your audience is and what they need from you.

Distill the knowledge into its simplest themes, free from jargon and hyperbole.

Test understanding of the message by asking stakeholders how it resonates with them.

Making knowledge actionable

Tom, a very successful life insurance executive, leads a large team of salespeople across the country. He knows he and his teammates are enthusiastic about the service they provide in every detail, but most prospective clients they meet are not.

When an advisor starts a conversation about intricacies of insurance coverages and fine differences between whole life versus variable life products, prospects are prone to lose interest. Tom has a wonderful saying that exemplifies the idea of Merchandising Knowledge: "It's not what insurance is, it's what it does that matters." With that simple message as the starting point, Tom's salespeople engage in a conversation about *how* the purchase of insurance provides policy owners with benefits that matter.

If a prospect wants to go deep into details about provisions of different policies, the salesperson is ready to share all their knowledge; but the *power* is in merchandising the knowledge so that it matters to the prospect. Like with Tom's insurance advisors, consider how you can communicate the benefits of what your knowledge *does*, not just what it *is*.

Let your audience guide you

The idea of presenting knowledge in a concise, headline-based fashion inspired Microsoft PowerPoint. Developed in the mid-1980s by a company called Forethought, the program that became PowerPoint was originally designed to provide visuals for group presentations within business organizations.

An advisor to the design team told me the idea was to replace old-school overhead projections with a tool used like a highway billboard. Communicate a simple message, with a few words and perhaps a photo or a graphic, with a slide. The presenter would elaborate on the message, then let her audience ask questions to get more information on the topic covered. This principle applies to Merchandising Knowledge. Present a clear, simple headline or thesis statement, then let your audience point you to the additional information they need in order to understand your knowledge.

Engaging others in Merchandising Knowledge

Unless you're a scientist, Arthur Stanley Eddington isn't a household name to you. Eddington, a British astrophysicist in the early 1900's, published nearly two dozen books covering astronomy, physics and the philosophy of science. He had a remarkable academic career as Plumian Professor of Astronomy and Experimental Philosophy at Cambridge, where he researched, taught and served as director of the Cambridge Observatory.

During World War I, Eddington learned about a new concept called the General Theory of Relativity, developed by a little-known German physicist named Albert Einstein. Eddington drew from his scientific expertise to understand and interpret Einstein's work. The more he studied the Theory of Relativity, the stronger advocate he became for Einstein's work within Britain. From today's vantage point, it's hard to imagine a time when Einstein wasn't well known, but that was the case when he first published his seminal work.

In his BBC article, *The Man Who Made Einstein World-Famous*, author Matthew Stanley explained that Einstein's ideas were trapped by the blockades of the Great War and even more by the vicious nationalism that made "enemy" [German] science unwelcome in the UK. But Einstein and Eddington both believed that science should transcend divisions of war. Stanley said their partnership allowed relativity to leap the trenches and make Einstein one of the most famous people on the globe.

According to Stanley, Einstein was very lucky Eddington became his liaison in Britain. Eddington dedicated himself to championing Einstein to revolutionize the foundations of science and restore internationalism to scientists themselves.

Engaging others in Merchandising Knowledge helps cope with challenges associated with communications. Mechanisms for communication during World War I were very limited, but with Eddington's engagement, Einstein's work found its way to a much larger audience.

The same principle applies to merchandising your knowledge. Identify colleagues with an interest in the knowledge you want to communicate and enable them to become advocates for you. Make it easy for them to share the message by providing clear, simple points they can make their own. Whether you are introducing the next best idea since the Theory of Relativity or something completely different, expanding your message through the right messengers will raise the effectiveness of your Merchandising Knowledge.

Steps to practice in Merchandising Knowledge

1. Understand *where* the real power is distilled from knowledge.
2. Understand *how* to simplify your knowledge into its simplest form – a headline or thesis statement.
3. Practice making knowledge actionable and promote it to those who can benefit from its application.
4. Learn from others by identifying exemplars in knowledge simplification and communication, as well as the reactions to those who frequently use the "data dump" approach to oversharing.
5. Let your audience guide you to share more detailed information in areas they want to explore further when you share knowledge.

Chapter 5
Making Strategy Matter

The past few years, my wife and I took winter trips to Sedona, Arizona, a high desert town about a hundred miles north of Phoenix, known for its beautiful red rock canyons, vortexes and Native American history.

We enjoyed the city's cool vibe, charming restaurants and fun shops. One Mexican restaurant caught our attention during our first Sedona visit, so we make it a priority destination every time we're in town. The executive chef/owner creates unique entrees and desserts in the spirit of traditional Southern Mexican food then adds his special flare to each recipe to make his menu stand out.

On one visit to this restaurant, the chef stepped out of the kitchen to visit with guests as they dined. When he stopped at our table, I said, "Your food is amazing, and I'm equally impressed with how well your business operates. Everything appears to run smoothly, and the restaurant is filled with happy customers. What is the key to your success?"

"I'm really not much of a businessperson," he said. "I'm passionate about the food I make. I love to eat the meals I prepare, and I only make food I love. I hire people who share my passion for this food, then I pray every day that our customers will love what I make for them. That's our strategy."

As a professional strategist, I've fallen into the trap of thinking good strategy needs to be highly detailed. My first reaction to his comment: This is too simple. The more I thought about it, the more elegant I found his business strategy. The restaurant created a clear vision: *Create and serve food that customers love.* The tactics aligned precisely with the vision: Hire people who share the vision, reinforce the vision every day with the team as you refine and prepare the menu items, measure employees based on actions they take to fulfill the vision, and visit customer's tables regularly to ask how they like their food to test how effectively the restaurant executes toward the vision.

For the rest of that evening, hosts, servers, cooks and preparers in the kitchen, food runners and bussers demonstrated the strategy in action. They *owned* the strategy and made it clear they wanted to ensure we loved our food. I observed people Making Strategy Matter as part of their normal routine. My conversation with the restaurant owner reinforced the point: *When strategy is clear, it's easier for team members to play a role in fulfilling the vision.*

Executives frequently discuss and seldom fully understand organizational strategy. Some organizations make strategic design an exclusive corner office activity. Others take a more inclusive approach, gathering broad stakeholder input as raw material to contribute to a plan. Or, as in the restaurant example, the entrepreneur defines the strategy, builds from a passion for the product and shares the plan with their team. In every case, leadership makes successful strategy fulfillment a team sport, where the players relevance is clear and each person's role contributes to achieving the organization's vision. Strategy takes place *through* every person in an organization.

Making Strategy Matter emanates from ~~knowing your role in fulfilling the company's strategy. It means you operate from the mindset that your position in the company exists~~ for a ~~purpose aligned with the organization's strategy.~~ Making Strategy Matter happens when you ~~demonstrate a sense of ownership of activities in your area of responsibility and continually seek ways to enhance your performance in alignment with the organization's vision.~~ Unfortunately, in many cases, organizational strategy is not clear, fully communicated or distilled into individual job descriptions. If any of these scenarios describe your organization, take the opportunity to sleuth out the information you need to Make Strategy Matter.

Understanding your organization's strategy

Strategy creates a framework to make decisions and perform activities aimed at a specific target state. Most organizations set up a formal operating strategy, documenting what they do (mission), why they do it (purpose), and how they fulfill their mission (strategy). Companies that don't have a formal, documented strategy may have a policy or procedure manual which guides decisions and activities.

Three common expressions of organizational strategy are *Intentional Plan, Say vs. Do* and the *Aural Plan.* Knowing *how* your organization is expressing its strategy prepares you to ask conversation-starting questions to understand how your daily activities align with the plan; how to Make Strategy Matter through your actions.

Under the Intentional Plan approach, an organization mindfully designs its strategy based on its competencies, access to resources, and competitive environment. Activity execution closely aligns with the plan.

The Say vs. Do approach begins intentionally, then evolves to a place where company activities aren't guided by the plan and may not align with the vision (think New Year's resolutions by late January).

The Aural Plan is spoken over time, perhaps by the founder, but is not well documented and may not provide clear decision-making guidance for the business or through job descriptions.

If your organization operates under an Intentional Plan, your path to Making Strategy Matter is straightforward. Questions to consider discussing with your manager, senior managers or a board member include:

- Which elements of my role are most aligned with our department strategy and overall organizational strategy?
- In what areas has the company strategy evolved or changed that can inform me about how my activities should change over time?
- If you wrote my job description today, based on your understanding of the organization's strategy, what would you change?
- What other areas of the organization are changing today that might impact our strategy tomorrow?
- What factors outside our company do you believe will have the greatest impact on refining our strategy in the future?

These questions stimulate conversation about alignment of activities you engage in with the broader organization; the value is in the resulting conversation and knowing that *strategy only happens through people.*

McGill University strategy professor and author Henry Mintzberg describes "emergent strategy" as a set of actions or behaviors consistent over time that create a realized pattern not expressly intended in the original strategy plans. Dr. Mintzberg's concept suggests that an organization learns what works in practice over time. As a result, an evolved strategy emerges. Emergent strategy often becomes an underlying factor in a Say vs. Do environment. Conversely, Say vs. Do can also result from losing sight of or veering off course from the initial strategy.

One of my earliest consulting engagements involved a residential home builder that specialized in developing modestly priced single-family tract homes. For years, this Southern California company was successful and profitable. At my first meeting with company senior leaders, I asked about their strategy. The CEO told me they grew their company building *starter homes for starter families.* He took great pride in knowing that young families started their lives in homes that fit their budget and met their needs – homes his company built! The home builder created a thorough business plan supporting this vision.

Over a two-year period prior to my engagement, the company's performance results began to deteriorate. They engaged me to identify and address the root cause driving the decline in profitability, then determine what strategic changes needed to take place.

During a growth cycle in the real estate market, the company noticed a trend taking place in Nevada and Arizona. Affluent Californians migrated to those states and bought larger, more upscale homes than they owned when they lived in the Golden State. Because prices for tract homes in California were relatively high, people could sell an existing home in that state, net a large equity profit, buy a custom home in a neighboring state with cash, and still have money left over. These California migrants became known as *equity bandits*.

The home builder interpreted this migration and the demand for upscale, custom homes as a market expansion opportunity. They decided to enter the custom home market outside Las Vegas in Henderson, Nevada. The company identified a prime location for development, bought undeveloped land, and jumped into the custom home market segment.

The firm built homes on speculation, investing its own money in the developments in anticipation of qualified buyers for the completed products, a new approach for this company. In all previous tract home developments, they started with buyers under contract committed to purchasing houses and used those contracts as collateral to borrow money for home construction.

In a short time, the home builder learned that architects who designed custom homes operated in a different manner than those they worked with in the tract home segment. With tract homes, they built hundreds of homes from a few basic designs; like making different-shaped cookies with two or three simple cookie cutters. In the custom space, each home's architectural design started from scratch. Custom homes required different materials than those sourced through their existing tract home vendors, so they had to identify new suppliers. Subcontractors also took a different approach from those used in the California tract home segment. The further the company got into building custom homes, the more they had to change the way they did business.

After I read the home builder's business plan and studied their financials, I saw they had drifted from their stated strategy. Following some preliminary analysis, I focused on three fundamental questions with management:

- What do custom home buyers expect and how does that differ from entry-level tract home buyers' expectations?
- What are your company's core competencies (what do you do exceptionally well), and how do those competencies apply in each of your market segments (tract and custom)?
- How do these two segments differ in terms of allocating your resources – people, time, capital?

Answers to these questions and the deeper conversations that followed made it clear this company was *executing a strategy they had not planned*. Market expansion is not bad; it's a necessary growth strategy for many businesses. However, in this case, when they stepped into custom home building on speculation, they entered a completely different business with different customers, different expectations, different vendors, different economics and no refined strategy. This case is the quintessential Say vs. Do strategy.

If you work in a Say vs. Do environment, your discussion questions should center on *interpreting actions* that describe the strategy in practice. In the homebuilder example, interpreting actions implies a blended low-cost provider and high value-added strategy; difficult to successfully execute. Most companies choose one or the other approach. Questions to ask of management to interpret the Say vs. Do strategy include:

- Who are our customers and what do they expect?
- Who are our suppliers and how do they align with our strategy?
- If we were to rewrite our strategy today based on the way the organization has evolved, how would you describe it?
- What are the most important elements of my role in supporting the strategy of our organization?
- Are other areas of the organization going through changes today that might impact our emerging strategy tomorrow?

The third common expression of an organization's strategy is the Aural Plan. Exemplified by the executive chef and owner of the Sedona Mexican restaurant, the crafter of the strategy communicates the Aural Plan by word of mouth to the people fulfilling the activities. This strategic approach is more prevalent in smaller companies and nonprofit organizations. In fulfillment mode, the Aural Plan can look like the Say vs. Do approach. Since the plan generally has no documentation, the Aural approach can either intentionally evolve or bob-and-weave based on management's fancy. Questions with the Aural Plan have similarities to the Say vs. Do approach in terms of serving to interpret how (or in some cases, if) actions align with the strategy.

- Who are our customers and what do they expect?
- Is the company anticipating changes in the customers we serve, and if so, what will those changes look like?
- If we were to document our strategy today based on the way the organization operates, how would you describe it?

- Who are your suppliers and how do they align with your strategy?
- How do you see my role in supporting the strategy of your organization?
- What factors outside of the organization do you see having the greatest impact on how we operate going forward?

The input from these organizational strategy descriptions and accompanying questions help guide you to make a meaningful impact in your work by Making Strategy Matter through your actions.

Interpreting and aligning your work with strategy

Notwithstanding the volumes written and taught and all the consulting and management dialog on the topic, few organizations are exemplars of strategy fulfillment. You can make a difference through conversations that follow your curiosity and inquiry, and mindfully align your work with the organization's strategy to the best of your ability. Not every person in the company *creates* the strategic plan, but everyone has a role in its fulfilment.

As a leader, you share *connection recognition* responsibility for understanding why your organization does the things it does, from a deductive point of view (big picture down to the details) and inductively (from details up to the big picture). When you make strategy an ongoing dialog rather than an annual or occasional event, you play an active role in bringing your company's vision to life by aligning your actions with where the organization wants to go.

Contributing to strategy fulfillment and evolution

Every person in an organization plays a role in Making Strategy Work. The vision comes to life when you understand the strategy, interpret how the macro-level plan distills into your daily activities, then bring your experience and organizational vantage point into the process. Every role in the organization has some connection to customers, vendors, regulators, competitors, industry organizations and data. Whatever your position in the organization, you can be a subject matter expert in at least two areas - *strategy fulfillment* as it relates to *your responsibilities*, and *your company* overall. Organizations often talk about empowering employees to do their jobs but seldom offer suggestions about how. When you practice the principles discussed in this chapter, you position yourself to demonstrate *empowerment* through the application of perspectives and experience you bring to strategy fulfilment.

Steps to practice in Making Strategy Matter

1. Be clear on your organization's strategy, vision, priorities and intentional activities.
2. Understand how your role supports the overall strategy; if it's unclear to you, ask.
3. Assure the aspects of your work which are within your control align with the organization's strategy.
4. Identify opportunities to contribute to the evolution of your organization's strategy through your work and recognition of cross-company connection points.
5. When you observe activities taking place in the organization that don't appear to align with the strategy, ask about them.

Chapter 6
Defining Your Story

Defining your Story is personal brand management that begins when you create a clear picture of your competencies, strengths, what you can contribute to your organization and how you want to be seen.

In the corporate world, the science of brand management offers principles which apply to managing your personal brand. Northwestern University professor Dr. Sean Gresh said corporate branding shows what companies stand for. The brand reflects how a company acts, how it serves people, the values the company shares, and how the company projects those values. The best brands tell their story in a simple manner that resonates with their audience.

In applying these principles to individuals, Dr. Gresh said a *personal brand* is similar to a corporate brand; it reflects who you are, what you stand for, the values you embrace, and the way you express those values. A company's brand helps communicate its value to customers and makes it stand out from competitors. A personal brand does the same for individuals, helping communicate a unique identity and clear value to potential employers or clients. Personal branding *is* your story.

Developing your personal brand requires you to step outside yourself and understand how others see you. When you expand self-awareness through understanding how you show up to others, you position yourself to contrast the observer's view with your self-perception, make conscious adjustments for personal growth and frame your story. The objective is to know yourself well, highlight your strengths, mitigate your challenges, and weave it all into your personal brand and story.

With your brand defined, you manage your story by consistently making prudent decisions aligned with it and demonstrating right actions which strengthen your leadership acumen and influence. Consistently showing-up *on brand* strengthens your reputation and trustworthiness.

In her book, *Nobody Understands You and What to Do About It*, social psychologist Heidi Grant says, "While the way people judge others may seem random, there are common thought processes underpinning our judgments, including biases, assumptions, and stereotypes. Understanding these processes is a first step in changing others' perceptions about us."

Grant explains that human beings perceive one another utilizing two thought phases. Phase One thinking is *unconscious and automatic*. It's based on what the mind takes in and is heavily influenced by unconscious assumptions. This type of thinking allows people to make sense of the world around them, but also leads to significant misjudgments. Phase Two thinking is *conscious* and involves an intentional analytical process. With Phase Two thinking, perceivers see assumptions, biases, and stereotypes and seek understanding beyond what they overtly perceive. In this arena of conscious thought, we can influence perceptions of ourselves that we want others to see.

Managing your brand requires you to *authentically* represent your competencies and how you contribute to the organization and at the same time demonstrate an awareness that you can shape others' perspectives of *you*. Intentionally, authentically shaping perspectives is the purpose of branding. When corporate brands become mere marketing slogans, people see through them in the blink of an eye. The same authenticity threshold holds true for individuals.

Dr. Ronald Riggio, professor at the Kravis Leadership Institute at Claremont-McKenna College wrote, "Impression management is very important in the development and maintenance of social relationships, and it is critically important to effectiveness as a leader. But success in social relationships and success as a leader requires a delicate balance of impression management. We need to monitor and control how we appear to others, but we also want to be straightforward and authentic."

Riggio offers six guidelines for managing the impressions we make on others in an authentic way:

1. *Know Thyself.* Self-awareness is critically important in successful impression management and in being an authentic person. It is important to have a sense of self - Who are you? What do you value? What do you stand for? – to avoid becoming a "social chameleon" who tries to fit in with the crowd.

2. *Be Thoughtful and Prudent.* You need to engage your brain when interacting with others. You must be an effective listener and try to understand others' points of view. You need to think

about the consequences of your statements and actions. Self-disclosure is an important part of forming good relationships with others, but you need to be careful to not disclose too much information too fast, and always consider how the other person reacts to what you tell them.

3. *Master Your Emotions.* Nothing creates a negative impression faster than an inappropriate emotional outburst. Emotions are important in connecting with others, but you need to regulate and moderate your emotions and your emotional displays. Negative affect – anger, irritation, disgust – should always be displayed carefully and strategically. For leaders, it is critically important to show emotional restraint, but to subtly let others know when you are pleased or displeased.

4. *Observe Rules of Etiquette.* To maintain a positive impression, it is critical to follow social norms and demonstrate that you have manners and know how to behave in different situations. Being polite is always a good impression management strategy.

5. *Have Courage and Conviction.* At times you need to be socially bold and courageous. Take the initiative to start a conversation with a stranger, ask a good question, or aid someone in distress. In addition, stand up for principles you believe in, particularly in positions of leadership. Most people will respect you for being true to your convictions.

6. *Be Positive.* A wealth of research supports the importance of positive affect in making good impressions. A smile and positive energy always work better than a negative tone.

Optimistic leaders who display positive affect are rated as more effective by their followers.[3]

Being genuine, knowing who you are and sharing yourself in the best light possible is authentic. Conversely, playing a role for the sake of creating a perception is fake, easily detected and unsustainable. Inauthenticity creates a lack of trust that makes it difficult to develop relationships. Authenticity requires vulnerability and taking the risk that others may not agree with you or like you - essential conditions in defining and demonstrating a believable, engaging personal brand.

Developing a personal value proposition

My daughter majored in theater in college. When we explored college options with Nicole, we visited different schools and sat in on classes to get a feel for how the program aligned with her interests.

On a visit to California State University, Fullerton, we observed a Broadway casting director give a guest lecture in an acting class. The director invited each student to present a three-minute sample of themselves and their craft. The director explained that students could do a monologue, sing a song, dance, or do a stand-up comedy routine. After each student performed, she spent a minute or two providing feedback as if she were casting a Broadway show; candid, unvarnished and in some cases, abrupt commentary.

---

[3] Psychology Today Posted 10/25/13 - The Dangerous Art of Impression Management: How to balance authenticity, tact, and common sense. https://www-Psychology Today-com.cdn.ampproject.org/c/s/www.psychologytoday.com/ca/blog/cutting-edge-leadership/201310/the-dangerous-art-impression-management?amp

After the first two performances, she paused the third student before he opened his mouth to sing and said, "Hold on. I want you to tell me why I should hire you. There will be five hundred other talented, well-educated and highly trained actors in line, auditioning for the same part you want, so I want you to tell me why I should hire you! Give me your *personal value proposition.*"

The young man stopped in his tracks. He looked confident when he stepped onto the stage for his turn with the director, but when she asked for his personal value proposition, I saw his confidence turn to fear. Prior to that moment, I suspect he defined his story as a talented, hard-working actor, working for his big break. After hearing the casting director's request, he looked lost. He needed to define his story to explain what he would contribute to a show and why the director should choose him.

After he developed his personal value proposition, the student might have said, "I combine my bi-cultural roots with extensive training and experience in live theater to bring dramatic material to life on stage. My vocal range and comfort across different musical styles helps me take on roles in classical musical theater as well as current popular plays."

With this type of personal value proposition, the casting director would have learned about how this auditioner differentiated himself and feel intrigued to hear more.

The value proposition puts your personal brand into words by articulating a clear picture of your competencies and strengths, what you contribute to your organization and how you want to be seen. Your personal value proposition must:

- Be simple, clear and concise.
- Personal and authentic.

- Explain the value you bring to your role and to the organization.
- Answer the question, "Why you?"

Your wording needs to reflect your communication style and be natural to who you are. Here are some examples of personal value propositions:

I use my deep experience and asset management knowledge to help families bring their financial plans to life. (investment manager)

My teammates and I work together to help our patients live their best lives every day. (family physician)

I am bilingual - fluent of the language of developers and consumers – which allows me to translate customer needs into business requirements that focus our product development activities. (tech company product management leader)

I help business development professionals create opportunities, add value throughout their sales cycle and close important deals. (sales manager)

I work with clients to define, design and deliver their organization's vision. (my consulting business personal value proposition)

You can use your personal value proposition in conversation with colleagues, customers, vendors and other professional relationships. It delivers the most impact as a natural part of a conversation or in a presentation. The more you practice articulating your value proposition, the more unrehearsed it will feel. This is your opportunity to communicate your brand and how you want to be seen, so make it count!

How do you reframe a story you haven't defined?

I worked as a bank utility clerk in college. The title – *utility clerk* - sounded exciting when I applied for the job. Once I started my position, I learned that "utility" meant I would be assigned all the tasks no one else wanted to do: Sorting checks, filing reports, organizing the regional stock room, filling in for tellers when they were on vacation, and occasionally helping the pest control people manage the branch's rodent problem. Utility clerk also meant that if another bank branch in the area was short-handed, I would fill in.

I worked in Los Angeles, and Fridays were always busy days at the bank. One Friday morning, I was asked to fill-in at a branch in Lynwood, five miles from my office. The Lynwood branch had three employees call in sick that morning, so I was asked to fill in as a teller. I spent the morning on the teller line, cashing checks, taking deposits and accepting payments. By midday, customer traffic slowed down, and I was released to go back to my branch.

I drove between these two bank branches frequently and knew a backstreet shortcut that saved time. As I made my way across Santa Ana Boulevard, approaching my branch at 103rd and Central, I saw two police cars rapidly approaching in my rearview mirror.

A thought flashed through my mind: I must have been speeding. My eyes lasered in on the speedometer to see how fast I drove. Before I could slow down, one of the police cars pulled in front of me, while the second car closed in on my rear bumper. Over the loudspeaker I heard a stern voice say, "Pull over and stop your car immediately." I felt my heart start pounding and thought *they really take speeding seriously on this stretch of road.*

I pulled to the side of the road, parked my car and reached to my back pocket to get my driver's license. As I moved my right hand toward the wallet in my pocket, again I heard the loudspeaker from the police car say, "Put your hands up and get out of the car *now!*"

They've got to be kidding! All this for a speeding ticket? I couldn't believe they wanted me to get out of the car for this. I couldn't have been going more than five miles an hour above the limit!

I opened the door, swung around and stood up to see two officers behind my car with their guns drawn and pointed at me. The next words were, "Turn facing your car. Put your hands on the roof. Make it slow and easy and you won't get hurt." At this point my sardonic sense of amusement with the situation turned to intense fear.

I didn't move a muscle. I was so scared, I'm not sure I was even breathing. Two officers approached me as a third opened the passenger door of my car.

I took a deep breath and got the courage to ask, "Do you mind telling me what's going on?"

"Shut up and don't move. We'll ask the questions." I followed orders and stood with my hands on the car. Next, an officer searched me, head to toe. Meanwhile, another officer took the keys from the ignition, opened the trunk and searched.

"Why are you here?" The officer's voice was intimidating.

"I'm working."

"Where do you work and why were you driving down this street in the middle of the day?"

I said, "I'm a bank utility clerk, and sometimes I travel between branches to help where I'm needed."

At this point, the situation de-escalated. The two officers with their guns drawn holstered their weapons and took a more relaxed stance. After checking my identification, calling my manager to verify my employment, an exhaustive search of my car and me, the lead officer said, "Thank you for your time. You can go now."

"Wait a minute, guys. Would you please tell me what just happened?" They couldn't just walk away after this intense experience without an explanation.

The lead officer said, "There was just a robbery at a liquor store two blocks from here. The robber was a tall male with light-colored complexion, and you are the first guy we saw that fit the description."

Wrong place, wrong time. I got pulled into a story that had nothing to do with me. I happened to be in the area while the experience unfolded.

It happens. You get pulled into a story that's not yours. A series of events or an intentional agenda creates a storyline which influences perceptions among your stakeholders. If it's a good story, you smile and carry on with your business. What if the story is unpleasant, untrue, or unrelated to you? What if you happen to be in the wrong place at the wrong time and get pulled into someone else's story?

These situations place you in a position you didn't choose yet provide an opportunity to practice *Leading from Where you Are*. To move quickly from frustration about being pulled into someone else's story, shift your mindset. These perspectives have worked for me and with people I've coached to make the needed mental shift into productive action:

Recognize that factors beyond your control can interfere with your story – If you can't avoid being pulled into a story that's not yours, you *can* take ownership of resolution.

Asking "why" isn't always productive – If knowing *why* something happened won't make a difference in how the issue is addressed, don't invest time and energy on the question.

Managing your brand is equally important when things are going as expected and when they're not – It's easy to withdraw or avoid dealing with events that challenge our brand; to proactively address the concern is a much better approach.

How we handle a negative situation is completely within our control – While we can't always change our circumstances, we get to choose how to deal with them; complaining about the condition is of no value, so determine how to accept the issue and elevate your story.

Situation management

In the *Apollo 13* movie, Tom Hanks delivered the classic line, "Houston, we have a problem."

At that point in the space mission, a major problem occurred on the Apollo spacecraft, but neither the astronauts nor mission control in Houston knew the magnitude of the issue. Although many tense moments passed during that mission, the astronauts and Houston eventually resolved the issues, and the Apollo 13 crew returned to earth safely.

Most of the everyday business challenges we encounter are nothing like those which surfaced during the Apollo 13 mission. However, unexpected situations arise and require a shift from proactive to reactive story definition.

November 1st was a Saturday morning. I sat in the barber chair getting a haircut when I received a text from one of the risk management people on my team at the bank. The message simply said, "Urgent situation, call ASAP."

I had no idea why Carter needed to talk, but this was the first time I received a message like that from him. I stepped outside the barber shop to call him to find out the problem. He said that overnight, a moderately severe system malfunction in another part of the bank affected our division's ability to accurately display client investment management account balance information online.

Carter discovered that instead of current account balance information, the information presented online defaulted to the prior month-end account statement; in this case data as of September 30th. A lot can happen over 31 days in a clients' investment account, which meant some clients would see overstated balance information while others would see understated values. Those inaccuracies could lead to significant problems in terms of a client's experience with our company and financial decision making. We needed to address the issue and communicate to all relevant parties expeditiously.

Over the course of the next hour, Carter learned that the underlying system issue which caused this online problem would most likely not be resolved until midday Sunday. With this information, we pulled together a conference call with my direct reports, our public relations department and a representative from the systems area in the part of the bank where the problem started.

We decided we needed to develop a message to post to clients' online accounts explaining that due to a systems issue within the bank, current account balance information was temporarily unavailable, and the info they saw online and through mobile devices reflected the September end-of-month balance. We provided a direct phone number to speak to an informed representative who could answer questions about the situation, and communicated with all client service officers in our division of the bank to let them know what happened, when the issue would be resolved and who they could speak with if they had additional questions. We also circulated the message to other leaders in the company, including the CEO, so everyone had full awareness of the issue and resolution plan.

In this situation, Carter and team got ahead of the story, laid out the facts, defined the situation quickly and communicated thoroughly. It could have turned out differently. Carter might have said, "It's Saturday morning and I don't want to bother people at home. I'll wait to see if the problem gets fixed."

That decision might have resulted in a handful of clients viewing their accounts online, noticing something wasn't right, and creating concern, anger or fear that the bank lost their money.

Fortunately, Carter, a mindful employee, intentionally choose to gather and share facts quickly and define the story before the story defined the bank. As a result, no clients raised concerns or filed complaints before the bank resolved the underlying problem.

Proactive messaging and managing your personal brand are valuable, intentional strategies to help you be seen the way you want to be seen within your organization. But what happens when an unexpected event occurs which requires you to *react*? How do you manage your message when something goes wrong? Here are a few simple guidelines for dealing with unplanned, unexpected, urgent events:

Understand what happened, including the root cause of the issue if possible.

Gather all the facts you can as quickly as possible, assemble them into a simple story to make it easy to understand for others who may not be steeped in the specific topic, and draw from the Merchandising Knowledge principles (distill the facts into their simplest form – a headline or thesis statement if possible).

Escalate through your management structure. (your manager or board and above; your team if appropriate).

Communicate to all relevant stakeholders as clearly and concisely as possible when information is shareable.

Engage other departments within your organization if appropriate (public relations, communications, customer service, legal, other impacted groups).

Test awareness of the communications surrounding the issue by asking colleagues or other stakeholders to share their understanding of the situation.

Repeat messaging through available channels if necessary, to assure you communicate the story effectively.

Steps to practice in Defining Your Story

1. Understand that Defining Your Story is *personal brand management.*
2. Develop a clear picture of your strengths, what you contribute to your organization and how you want to be seen.
3. Define your personal value proposition and become competent in knowing when and how to use it authentically.
4. Identify opportunities to build your personal brand.
5. Be prepared to navigate unexpected situations requiring a quick reaction.

Chapter 7
The Power of Enthusiasm

One of the richest times in my career for learning, growing and testing my mettle as a leader came during the 2008 – 2009 financial crisis. I worked for a national bank and headed one of the largest fiduciary asset management businesses in the country. My business served affluent individuals, most of whom spent their lives creating wealth through entrepreneurial activities as small business owners, company founders and corporate executives. They invested in financial assets – equities, bonds, and real assets, which comprised a substantive part of their net worth.

In the financial crisis era, U.S. equity markets lost half their value between October 2007 and March 2009. Fear among investors ran extremely high, and what happened in the economy rattled main street Americans. Unemployment peaked at 9.5% in 2009.

Record numbers of homeowners defaulted on their mortgages, leading to historic rates of home foreclosures. The financial services industry suffered frequent bank failures, government takeovers and mergers. I worked for a financially sound and quite strong firm, and as a result, we acquired a bank equal to our size at a fire-sale price.

In those chaotic days, I spent time with my team members helping maintain confidence in the United States financial system, reassuring clients that things would eventually stabilize, leading my business through the largest merger of its kind ever, and working with regulators and the government to interpret what was happening and why, and how to avoid it in the future. I worked twelve-hour days and filled my nights and weekends with special projects. Some days were draining, and at the same time, exhilarating.

I rarely took a lunch break, but one challenging day, I needed to get outside my office and breathe fresh air. The morning started with a major water main break at one of my facilities in Nevada, causing us to shut down service at that location.

At the same time, a system outage in the Midwest impacted thousands of clients. While navigating both those events, I spent four hours on a conference call with regulators. By midday, I reached my capacity for issues, so I went for a walk to pick up lunch.

My office was located next to the city bus station. As I walked to a take-out restaurant down the street, I noticed a middle-aged man sitting at the bus stop with a big smile on his face, pointing at me.

I didn't know what he was smiling about, but he got up from the bench, approached me, beaming and anxious to talk.

"Have you ever seen that movie called Trading Places with Eddie Murphy and Dan Ackroyd?"

I said, "Sure, I saw it a long time ago. Good movie. Why do you ask?"

"The story is about this hustler from the streets who trades places with a businessman – I think he was an investment guy - who worked for a big bank in Philly."

I told him I remembered the storyline.

"You remind me of the banker, and I remind myself of the Eddie Murphy character. Kind of funny, right?"

I didn't think he looked much like Eddie Murphy and I don't look like Dan Ackroyd. I happened to be wearing a pin-striped suit that day and apparently looked like a banker, so I said, "I suppose I can see that."

At that moment, I wasn't particularly interested in talking about old movies. I wanted to get lunch, clear my head and go back to the office. Out of frustration with my work, I said, "I don't know what your job is, but I can't imagine you'd want to trade places with me today."

Without missing a beat, he said, "Sir, I would trade jobs with you any day of the week, including today!"

That friendly stranger's words hit me like a ton of bricks. He shifted my perspective about the day, the drama and feeling sorry for myself. That single sentence pulled me out of my funk, helped me feel more enthusiastic about my work and shifted my focus to why it mattered. I'm sure it was nothing more than fun banter on his part; no serious intent. But the authentic enthusiasm he demonstrated when he offered to *trade places* with me caused me to step away from my own pity party and recognize that my attitude is my choice. I could decide to be optimistic, even enthusiastic, when I needed to be.

That day I wasn't serving anyone well – my team members, clients or regulators – by focusing on the things that frustrated me. Yes, I could rationalize feeling unhappy about all that was going on; we're all entitled to experience our feelings. But I needed to demonstrate leadership in my work. That doesn't mean denying reality; it means recognizing my ability to choose a different mindset.

Meeting that man on the street changed my demeanor for the day and many days to follow. It helped me see no matter how challenging my days felt, someone would always gladly trade places given a chance. I learned a valuable lesson about choosing my frame of mind, including the choice of enthusiasm when necessary.

Ralph Waldo Emerson wrote, "Enthusiasm is one of the most powerful engines of success. Be active, be energetic, be enthusiastic and faithful, and you will accomplish your objective. Nothing great was ever achieved without enthusiasm."

It feels good to be around enthusiastic people. When someone is enthusiastic about a topic, their energy pours into those around them. Enthusiastic leaders set the tone for their teams and define an expectation of optimism.

Managing your enthusiasm

Our level of enthusiasm impacts the people around us. Think about people you work with and how their level of enthusiasm (or lack thereof) for a new project or idea affects you. The case for enthusiasm is compelling but can you *choose* to be enthusiastic? Can you *manage* your level of enthusiasm? In the words of one of my early mentors, *"You're either fired with enthusiasm; or, you're fired...with enthusiasm."*

My mentor and many researchers believe people can manage enthusiasm levels to fit a specific situation. That doesn't mean you fake your reactions or pour on artificial charm to sell an idea. Instead, managing enthusiasm means you're *mindfully focusing authentic energy into supporting an idea.* This definition presupposes you can harness your inner excitement for an idea, a project or a proposal by drawing on the natural energy the topic evokes in you.

Fortunately, we are all wired differently. By nature, some people are more expressive and demonstrating enthusiasm is second nature to them. For others, displaying enthusiasm is a conscious action. Whichever category you fall into, it's important to know why, when and how to demonstrate enthusiasm.

Why

Intentionally managing enthusiasm is a strategy for emphasizing your views on an idea, a cause or project you can influence. This does not replace naturally occurring enthusiasm; rather it mindfully adds an exclamation point at the end of a sentence! This strategy includes consciously drawing on your non-verbal communication skills to emphasize your point. When we want to make an important point, we cannot rely on our words alone.

When

In tenth grade, I was one of three guitar players in my high school's jazz band. The other guitarists, Brian and Robby, were seniors when I was a sophomore. Both were outstanding musicians. Most of the time I played rhythm parts while one of the other two guitarists would be assigned solo parts.

When we returned to school after the holiday break during my tenth-grade year, Robby showed up to jazz band rehearsal with a Cry Baby wah-wah pedal he received as a Christmas present. The wah-wah pedal is a sound effect guitar players use to change the tone of their instrument. Rotating the pedal up and down with your foot creates a *wah-wah* sound, like the guitar is crying.

Robby connected the new Cry Baby pedal to his guitar, turned on the amplifier, then let it rip. He demonstrated just how cool the wah-wah effect sounded. The tones he created blew me away; he sounded even more like a professional than he did before he got his new pedal.

A few minutes after Robby's impromptu demonstration, jazz band rehearsal started. Robby used the wah-wah on his solos. Then, he used it when he played his rhythm parts. Sometimes, he used it in between songs because he liked the sounds he could make. The wah-wah sound captured the attention of people in our jazz band that first day after winter break. On the second day of rehearsal, Robby's continuous wah-wahing lost some of its charm. By day three, it got annoying because Robby wah-wahed every time he played. In fact, it wasn't long before the jazz band teacher asked Robby to stop using the wah-wah pedal because it became a distraction.

The problem: when Robby used the wah-wah pedal *all the time*, it no longer *highlighted* a note or feeling he wanted to accentuate. It became the norm and didn't stand out. The same concept applies to intentionally using enthusiasm as a communication strategy. For the greatest impact, *intentional enthusiasm needs to be used to highlight and accentuate your message* when you identify a cause you authentically support.

Authenticity is essential; anything less than belief in the idea or initiative you plan on supporting will not serve the organization or you. If you cannot *authentically* feel the internal energy required to manifest enthusiasm, wait for another opportunity to deploy this communication strategy.

We need to go along with some company decisions even when we do not *enthusiastically* support them. With the caveat that your company engages in ethical, legal and compliant activities, supporting a management decision you might not love is part of organizational life. Going along with the program when it's necessary requires the practice of a different strategy - *humble acceptance.*

How

Drawing on your inner reservoir of authentic enthusiasm starts with carefully reading the environment within which you work. Determine whether intentional enthusiasm is appropriate. When you're in a situation that lends itself to demonstrating enthusiasm, consider these seven actions to help you put this energy into practice:

- When you feel passion for a topic, harness the energy and let it show. Many people were taught to minimize emotions or hide feelings in a business setting, so this step may feel uncomfortable. Keep in mind that this action simply allows colleagues to see the energy within.
- Focus on *why* this cause, idea or project is important to *you,* then articulate that impetus.
- Stay positive, even if you use enthusiasm to present a position against a proposal. This means you present an alternative idea or recommendation without criticizing another position.
- Check your *purpose* before speaking. Make sure you come from a place of authenticity when you express your enthusiasm. If you make a better outcome for the organization your purpose for enthusiastically

espousing an idea, this communication strategy will have more impact.

- Take three deep breaths to center yourself, then align your energy level with an enthusiastic message. Breathe deep to calm yourself, lower stress and focus your energy.
- Manage your physical presence. Sit straight if you're seated, stand tall if you're standing, and lean in as you speak. Make engaging eye contact and use hand and facial gestures that help express your enthusiasm.
- Believe your voice matters. You joined your organization to make an impact. Enthusiastically presenting or supporting an idea is part of the way your work makes a difference.

Steps to practice in the Power of Enthusiasm

1. Observe the impact and influence of people you work with who demonstrate high levels of enthusiasm.
2. Be clear about the impact your enthusiasm has on the people you work with.
3. Understand what it takes for you to draw on your inner reservoir of authentic enthusiasm.
4. Identify the most impactful opportunities to demonstrate your enthusiasm.
5. Monitor yourself to identify times when your enthusiasm doesn't match the needs of the situation; adjust accordingly.

Chapter 8
Applying the Themes

William James, Harvard professor, from 1872 to 1907, considered the Father of American psychology, said "Act as if what you do makes a difference. It does.". James also said, "Human beings, by changing the inner attitudes of their minds, can change the outer aspects of their lives."

Leading from Where you Are posits leadership as a set of conscious choices and behaviors. When you *intentionally* define and mindfully display how you show up in your work, you manage your professional presence and assure the role you play in your work makes a difference. These seven themes provide content to build and implement your personal operating strategy.

Your strategy for *Leading from Where you Are*

I love to develop, implement, evaluate effectiveness, and refine strategy. I read about the topic frequently, I write about it, I focused on it in graduate school, and I taught a college course on strategic management. Notwithstanding this background, one of my most valued strategy lessons didn't come from business or academia. It came from my son when he attended middle school.

Michael joined the chess club at his middle school. He showed little interest in sports, but the game of chess excited him. The club helped him learn the fundamentals of the game and build competency. At home, we played chess together two or three times a week. He usually won. On those rare occasions when I emerged the victor, I suspected he threw the game to minimize bruising to my ego.

After dinner one evening, as he made his final move to win the third and final game of the night, Michael said, "Dad, the key to strategy in chess is always know your next set of moves."

What a simple, ideal metaphor for *all* strategy. Michael won the game and I scored a lesson I still apply today. A key to your professional strategy in *Leading from Where you Are* is always know your next set of moves to develop yourself, your competencies and the impact you have on your organization.

Understanding the seven themes you developed through this book prepares you to apply these ideas in your work. Each chapter includes five steps to practice the theme described. This chapter helps you define the set of moves to take next to bring the theme to life in your daily activities. Use these steps to develop your strategy:

- Develop a clear picture of the result you intend to create with a theme and how the theme applies to this result.
- Review the Steps to Practice each theme (summarized at the end of this chapter).
- Note the specific steps you'll take.
- Determine how, when and where you will apply each theme.
- Implement.

Create your individualized plan to make these ideas actionable in your professional life. The seven themes of *Leading from Where you Are* work together to optimize the role you play as a meaningful contributor of ideas, actions and engagement to your organization. The dynamics of who you are, where, and with whom you work will cause certain of these themes to resonate more profoundly than others. I recommend an initial focus on the top one or two themes that resonate most with you, likely to be *big rock* opportunities in your leadership journey.

Selecting your first focus theme

This book is a *practitioner's* guide, written with real world application of each theme in mind. As the practitioner, finding the right starting place comes from asking, *"Which of the seven themes stood out most to me as I read through them and why?"*

How you answer these questions will tell you the best theme to practice first.

For example, if you are preparing for a performance review with your manager and want to better align your daily activities with the company's strategy, Making Strategy Matter may be your starting place. If you recently joined the company, Proactive Relationship Management might be the right place to start. If you are developing a new idea for a product upgrade, the Power of Enthusiasm may be a great starting point.

Why not take on all seven themes together?

Taking on too much at once leads to inertia, where nothing happens. Think about the list of New Year's resolutions you created at the beginning of this year then forgot about by February 1st!

The seven themes in *Leading from Where you Are* build on each other to encourage micro progress and accretion of competencies. Practice and build competency one theme at a time and you will see your leadership fluency and your impact in your organization grow.

Defining expected results

For behavioral change to take root, you must build definition around an achievable future state. Clarify your expectations by asking yourself, *"What does success look like for me as I develop competency in a specific theme?"* If you selected the Power of Enthusiasm as your first theme, think about how you will intentionally express authentic enthusiasm. Define your purpose for demonstrating this theme. For example, to demonstrate intentional enthusiasm could garner support for implementation of a new idea. Then shift your attention to how you build competency in this theme over time. In the words of Stephen Covey, *begin with the end in mind.*

From Skill to Competency

Skills require practice to become *competencies. Skill* refers to the ability to perform a certain task. For a pianist, a foundational skill is learning to play the basic seven-note scales. *Competency* refers to proficiency in performing a skill. Performing a piece by Mozart requires a higher level of competency for the pianist than playing a basic scale.

The same concept works when you perform the themes in *Leading from Where you Are.* You need to practice your basic scales – the seven themes – over time to develop competencies. As with the developing piano player who works on her scales then performs at a recital, demonstrating proficiency in performing these leadership actions in your work is your *recital.*

Building competency

Competency results from regular practice of each theme's fundamentals. As you grow your competency, your leadership presence expands, and you develop new habits. Mindfulness matters. Remaining conscious of your intentional actions enables you to expand your proficiency.

Start small in developing your competency in *Leading from Where you Are.* Identify low-risk situations where you can practice a theme. Say you're practicing the Art of Inquiry. A low-risk situation could be to get to know a co-worker better. Start the process by developing three to five open-ended questions that give you the best insights into what matters most to this person, what they value, what concerns them in their work and what they like to do when they're outside of work.

Lisa, head of a large operations department, was one of my coaching clients. After six months in her new role, with a mandate to clean up operational and financial problems stemming from her predecessor, she felt concerned her team didn't accept her.

Feedback from Lisa's team said she was a "task master who only cares about results."

I asked how she felt about the perception.

"These people are misreading me and my style. They don't understand what's expected of me and our department. I care about my team and I care about results, but they don't see the other part of me."

I asked how her team members could know the *real* Lisa. As we discussed this, it became clear she never gave them an opportunity to *see* her. For a homework assignment, I asked Lisa to practice the Art of Inquiry. Together, we scripted two simple questions she'd feather into conversations with each of her direct reports when the appropriate opportunity arose. Lisa's questions were:

- "Since we're still getting to know each other, tell me about what first attracted you to come to work at our company?"
- "I see you work a lot of hours here every day. When you're in your car, driving home, what do you think about that tells you today was productive or not?"

These simple questions created a transformational impact on Lisa's relationships. She didn't change who she was; she practiced the Art of Inquiry to learn more about the people who worked on her team. Those two questions led to conversations which created the foundation for real relationships. Lisa's team members began to see her as the caring, engaging person she really is. This exercise provided a low risk, high return on Lisa's investment in developing competency in the Art of Inquiry.

Scouting the low-risk environment for experimentation

Consider yourself in the *research and development* phase of working with the seven themes. To identify opportune timing and find the right environment to demonstrate themes means you take a mindful approach. Low risk environments include small group meetings or informal project team settings. Large group meetings, highly structured sessions or events where senior leaders present ideas in a manner that discourages feedback are higher risk situations. Pick the right environment that minimizes down-side risk for you.

Performance self-evaluation

Self-evaluations have advantages and disadvantages. Advantages include ease of access to how you feel you've performed on a given theme, and immediate feedback. On the disadvantages list, people tend to be less objective with themselves (both, in terms of favorable and unfavorable assessments), and are more likely to be self-critical. As you evaluate your performance, keep in mind that you may be exaggerating points of criticism or praise. With that self-reminder, garner as much learning from the experience as possible.

Course corrections

The purpose of self-assessment and other feedback you receive on how you're *Leading from Where you Are* is to understand the observations, interpret them relative to specific actions, and adjust future actions accordingly. As you practice these themes, allow yourself to make mistakes, fall short of your own expectations or have a flat experience. Treat each of these outcomes as a learning experience that will inform development and growth in your leadership journey.

Conscious Choreography

Making conscious decisions to choreograph how you demonstrate your leadership presence is critical to *Leading from Where you Are*. This intentional approach may feel uncomfortable at first as human beings tend to make behavioral choices in the moment. Instead, you intentionally develop predetermined actions to fit an expected circumstance, are strategic and position you with a range of behavioral options you wouldn't otherwise have. It's much better to have a broad leadership repertoire available and ready to draw from than to be caught flat-footed in a situation and need to scramble for the right approach.

Predetermined actions bias us toward conscious, proactive decision making, a form of choreography, which means *the arrangement of actions leading up to and through an event.*

Planning actions in advance enables you to show up the way you intend. Consider your participation at a staff meeting. How could you develop choreographed moves in advance? If you receive an agenda before the meeting, study the topics and pick one point you can discuss. Ask yourself how you can practice The Art of Inquiry, Making Strategy Matter or any theme as part of the conversation on an agenda topic.

Absent preplanned leadership choreography, people go to a meeting and just react to the topics being discussed. Subconscious, reactive decisions differ from those anticipated in advance and risk creating suboptimal outcomes. Apply information you access in advance of a meeting, then read the situation in the moment for opportunities to contribute, enhance your participation in the conversation and influence outcomes.

Actions that define characteristics

Look at people in your organization and elsewhere who you consider leadership exemplars. What defines your perspective on these people? What characteristics express leadership acumen? Confidence, communication style, warmth, passion, authenticity? Demonstrating these characteristics results from a specific set of actions. Focus on defining *intentional actions* aligned with one of the seven themes to demonstrate leadership characteristics.

Gather intel to develop your choreography

Your diligence about when, where and how to exercise *Leading from Where you Are* themes provides a clear read on environmental factors that affect your implementation plan. What situation do you intend to engage in? How is it perceived by colleagues and management? What lightening rod issues must you avoid? What political dynamics show up? Understanding these environmental dimensions will guide you to define your approach to consciously choreograph how you show up in your work.

What's Next: Follow-on Themes

You've now practiced your first theme and are ready to expand your competency repertoire. For the next leg of your journey, prioritize your choices based on what will be most impactful to you. The *big rock* philosophy uses a metaphor which says if you want to fill a jar with rocks, and the goal is to fit as much material into the jar as possible, you start with the biggest rocks first. From there, you add the second largest rocks, then the third largest, and so on until the jar is full. Conversely, if you put sand and small stones in the jar first, there wouldn't be enough room to add the big rocks later. Translated, the metaphor means – tackle the most important, big issues first, then deal with the smaller things. The philosophy for working with the seven themes is the same – start with the most impactful themes first, then add material to your repertoire.

Choose the next most important theme

As you explore which next theme to practice, consider how it works with your first theme. If your first theme was Nurturing Ideation, Merchandising Knowledge is a logical next step as the two build on each other. Similarly, Proactive Relationship Management and The Art of Inquiry work the same way. Since all seven themes complement the others, you select the implementation order which works best for you.

As you build your acumen across all seven themes, one at a time, you will notice your confidence in *Leading from Where you Are* grows. Stay attuned to opportunities which create synergies through combining themes to grow your leadership acumen.

Get feedback from others

Effective feedback starts with making it easy for people to share their observations about your performance. A good way to do this is ask *specific* questions that help inform you about how you're doing with *Leading from Where you Are*. As you seek feedback, keep the outcomes you work toward in mind. Feedback helps you compare current outcomes with your development goals and adjust activities where you need to make course corrections.

When you work on Proactive Relationship Management, you might ask a colleague how they feel about the quality of conversations you share when you discuss a project you're working on together.

When her company promoted Anna from a regional job in the Southwest to a national position, her responsibilities increased, and her network expanded exponentially.

In her prior role, all of Anna's stakeholders – manager, direct reports, peers, customers – were in the same geographic area, with most people in the same building. Anna enjoyed strong, trusted relationships with coworkers who viewed her as a key leader in her business. Her new job involved a different set of colleagues, spread across the country. None of her new peers worked in Anna's office location. Anna's assistant was the only direct report based in her city. In her new position,

Anna worked with people in 20 cities across four time zones; people she would rarely see in person.

To proactively manage relationships, Anna developed a plan which included holding individual video or phone meetings with her closest stakeholders every other week. In her case, this group included her direct reports and peers. For colleagues in her second circle – people in other departments her team interacted with – Anna held monthly calls. For people who didn't cross her path frequently, she initiated a video meeting quarterly or whenever a specific topic of mutual interest arose.

Most of Anna's relationships in her national role were virtual, adding complexity to collaboration. To assure her colleagues got what they needed from the relationship, Anna asked for feedback. She learned she satisfied most of her stakeholders. One partner felt he didn't get the level of attention he expected and provided her with this feedback.

Anna asked, "What can I do to change our interactions?"

He said, "Stop by to meet with me in person the next time you're in the area. If we meet a couple of hours in person once a year, you'll know what's going on in my region, and I'll know what's important to you."

She made that simple adjustment and improved the nature of the relationship.

For most of us, trusting feedback we receive is subject to the trust we have in the relationship and how effectively we communicate. An exercise I find helpful in assessing communication effectiveness involves answering a three-question survey:

- Overall, how would you rate the effectiveness of our communications?

- How would you rate our effectiveness in surfacing and addressing issues or conflicts with each other?
- What level of candor do you feel we share in our communications?

You can ask and answer these questions with a colleague in person or via video. Each person writes their answers to the three questions on a Post-it Note and assigns a rating of 1-5, where 5 is Outstanding, 1 is Very Poor. The purpose of the exercise is to see how similar or divergent responses are, then delve into gaps and understand differences in perceptions. Working through this exercise requires candor; high scores are not as valuable to the relationship as honest feedback. This exercise surfaces strengths in a relationship as well as opportunities for improvement.

Receiving feedback well

In the words of Mick Jagger, "You can't always get what you want, but if you try sometimes, you just might get what you need!"

It feels good when we get the feedback we *want*. Positive feedback helps reinforce our efforts and satisfies our human need for recognition. Then there's the feedback we *need,* which may not feel quite as good.

Accurate feedback can be painful and trigger our *fight or flight* response to defend ourselves. When you ask for specific, actionable feedback, it's essential to mean it. Listen carefully to what you receive and be prepared to hear what you need.

Hearing feedback we don't like takes practice. Fighting the urge to correct misperceptions about the way we show up is critical. If we ask for feedback, then fall into a reactive mode of defense, no one will want to provide us with their observations in the future.

Giving good feedback can be difficult, so when you ask and receive actionable observations, empathize with the person who cared enough to share their perspectives. Hear the feedback, absorb it, deliberately process the perspectives, then ask yourself – what can I learn from what I've heard? Remember, it can be a challenge to give or receive feedback, and when you make it easy for those who to offer their observations, you open the door to greater personal growth.

Adjusting your approach

Early in my tenure as a manager, I received a 360-degree performance review. The review process integrated my self-assessment with feedback from my manager, five peers and all my direct reports. I read the first section of my review, which presented observations from my direct reports. Their comments pleased me. Next, I read my manager's feedback, which was also positive and encouraging. I really enjoyed the 360-degree feedback approach until I got to the section representing my peers.

I didn't identify with the term *Aloof*. But there it was in black and white. "Dave can come across as aloof and stand-offish. He never seems to have time for me."

I thought I received somebody else's report; they couldn't be talking about me. I considered myself friendly and engaging. I valued my relationships, regularly sent birthday cards, called for holidays and special events. I *knew* I was a people person, so the feedback must have been wrong. It turned out I was wrong.

I saw myself working and getting things done. Some of my peers read my task-orientation to mean I was distant or not interested in relationships. Unintentionally and unconsciously, I overlooked the fact that my sphere of professional *relationships* was larger than I thought. Even though my boss was pleased with my work, failing to connect and develop relationships more broadly could eventually impede my ability to get the job done.

Once I moved beyond my surprise and accepted the perceptions underlying the feedback, I worked on empathizing and understanding how I might have created these views. With that understanding, I adjusted my approach by developing a question I'd ask myself before meeting with peers: "What does this group or person need from me right now?" Do they need me to show up as an engaging co-worker, interested in them and part of a relationship, or, is driving a task to closure my role in this situation?

When I read the situation, then intentionally forged my approach to an interaction, I could determine how to best meet the needs of the specific situation and be seen the way I wanted to be seen. This behavioral tweak went a long way towards improving my relationships and the way my colleagues perceived me.

Feedback is most beneficial when it spurs self-reflection and behavioral adjustment. The feedback I heard helped me adjust my approach and raise my effectiveness.

Summary of Steps to practice *Leading from Where you Are*

Proactive Relationship Management

1. Intentionally block time on your calendar for Proactive Relationship Management time every week.
2. Identify the people in roles with the greatest relevance to your work and prioritize who you will engage and how often.
3. Be prepared with mindful conversation starters and conversation topics.
4. Recognize the importance of building and sustaining trust in relationships.
5. Understand how to practice realness in your relationships.

Mastering the Art of Inquiry

1. Recognize how authentic curiosity and Mastering the Art of Inquiry create the pathway to develop understanding, build meaningful relationships and expand knowledge.
2. Build a repertoire of open-ended purposeful questions to guide conversations.
3. Frame questions around points of curiosity that will contribute to a meaningful conversation.
4. Listen for invitations for follow-on questions.
5. Develop confidence in diplomatically asking *why* questions.

Nurturing Ideation

1. Recognize the iterative nature of ideation and consider how your individual competencies serve as ingredients that add to the process.
2. Identify those organization-wide activities closest to your work and be clear about how your work fits into the broader ecosystem of the company. From that vantage point, look at each touchpoint for improvement iterations and use this as inspiration for ideation.
3. Practice reading your environment for opportunities to offer new ideas or meaningfully add to the ideas of others. As with riffing in music, knowing when to float an idea can be as important as the idea itself.
4. Apply lessons from Mastering the Art of Inquiry to source invitations to contribute to ideation.
5. Demonstrate enthusiasm for the ideas you present while practicing non-attachment to the outcome.

Merchandising Knowledge

1. Understand *where* the real power is garnered from knowledge.
2. Understand *how* to simplify your knowledge into its simplest form – a headline or thesis statement.
3. Practice making knowledge actionable and promote it to those who can benefit from its application.
4. Learn from others by identifying exemplars in knowledge simplification and communication, as well the reactions to those who frequently use the "data dump" approach to oversharing.

5. Let your audience guide you to share more detailed information in areas they want to explore further when you share knowledge.

Making Strategy Matter

1. Be clear on your organization's strategy – it's vision, priorities and intentional activities.
2. Understand how your role supports the overall strategy. If it's unclear to you, ask.
3. Assure the aspects of your work which you control align with the organization's strategy.
4. Identify opportunities to contribute to the evolution of your organization's strategy through your work and recognition of cross-company connection points.
5. When you observe actions taking place in the organization that don't appear to align with the strategy, ask about them.

Defining Your Story

1. Understand that Defining Your Story is *personal brand management.*
2. Develop a clear picture of your strengths, what you contribute to your organization and how you want to be seen.
3. Define your personal value proposition and become competent in knowing when and how to use it authentically.
4. Identify opportunities to build your personal brand.
5. Be prepared to navigate unexpected situations requiring a quick reaction.

The Power of Enthusiasm

1. Observe the impact and influence of people you work with who demonstrate high levels of enthusiasm.

2. Be clear about the impact your enthusiasm has on the people you work with.

3. Understand what it takes for you to draw on your inner reservoir of authentic enthusiasm.

4. Identify the most impactful opportunities to demonstrate your enthusiasm.

5. Monitor yourself to identify times when your enthusiasm doesn't match the needs of the situation; adjust accordingly.

Chapter 9
Making an Impact

Meaning in our work comes from feeling we're making an impact through our ideas and actions. Financial rewards matter, yet research tells us, absent emotional fulfillment from participating in meaningful work, our *engagement* is at risk. The purpose of *Leading from Where you Are* is to empower you to optimize the impact you make in your organization, thereby increasing the meaning derived through your work.

I have focused so far on you and your contribution through your work, which represents one dimension of the *meaningful work* equation. The second dimension arises from the role your organization plays in making work matter. *Leading from Where you Are* themes are actions within *your* control, applied as you see fit. You expect your organization to operate ethically, inclusively, legally and in compliance with all applicable regulations - all non-negotiable attributes. Beyond these requirements, your preferred organizational characteristics may include a worthy mission, values that align with yours, engaging strategy, collaborative culture, career growth potential and a dynamic operating environment. What if your company doesn't satisfy all the attributes on your list?

Acceptance, influence or exit?

Our choices to address gaps between expectations of the organization and what the company demonstrates fall into three categories: acceptance of the gaps, influencing change that reduces or removes the gaps and exiting the organization in favor of an employer better aligned with our expectations. To assess which of these options is the best path for you begins with identification of the root cause of the difference. Are gaps due to intentional design or unrealized impacts? These situations illustrate both root causes:

- You value a collaborative environment. You work at a company that encourages competition among employees. This gap emanates from intentional design; the company intentionally created a culture to stimulate competition.

- You started a new job with a company based on your perception of the opportunity for career advancement. When you interviewed for the position, you were told the company strives to guide employees' personal development. Now, in the job, you ask *how* to access developmental experiences for advancement and learn the company doesn't have a formal approach to helping employees grow. This is an unrealized impact; not an intentional disconnect.

I was a senior vice president in Bank of America's international banking business when NationsBank merged with BofA. Both banks had deep roots in the industry. NationsBank was founded in 1874 as Commercial National Bank in Charlotte, North Carolina. In 1904, Bank of America opened in San Francisco, California as the Bank of Italy. Both banks grew organically and through acquisition. By 1998, when the banks announced the merger, the two companies were amalgamations of hundreds of smaller institutions.

Large mergers always cause cultural change in an organization. The changes at the new Bank of America were intentional. Hugh McColl, CEO of the combined company, said "If you've got a culture you wish to change you shouldn't leave any vestige of the old culture in existence. You must destroy the culture in its entirety."[4]

That is what happened.

The merged company culture became more NationsBank than legacy Bank of America and reflected a set of clear corporate values. Not a bad thing, but different from the culture to which I felt aligned. After a year of working through merger activities, I recognized that the culture of the new company didn't align with my interests.

Around that time, I attended a large group meeting where Hugh McColl spoke to employees. He complimented the group on progress bringing the two companies together, then said, "We have a clear path forward with the new Bank of America. The two legacy banks that existed before the merger are no more; we are one Bank of America. Our new company is like a train leaving the station. There's room for every one of you on this train, but if you don't like where we're going, it's time to step off."

---

[4] Banktown: The Rise and Struggle of Charlottes Big Banks by Rick Rothacker, (c) 2010, page 35

Mr. McColl's comments resonated with me. I could accept the new company's culture, or, in his words, step off the train. I valued his candor and clarity about the post-merger culture. With that insight I decided my path forward was to exit the company.

Acceptance of the environment, influencing change, or exiting are your options. Context for deciding which path to take includes recognition of your role in the company. Every organization is a community of individuals. Each, from entry-level employee to CEO, plays their own role in the company. This contextual awareness casts light on the "us and them" mindset; there is no "them", there is only "us." A company has different departments, divisions and levels of responsibility. When you work for that organization, *you are the company*. If the context doesn't feel right to you as you evaluate where you work, it's probably not the right place for you.

Lack of clarity about alternatives – acceptance, influencing change, or exiting – may be one factor contributing to the disengagement epidemic in the workplace today.

Gallup surveys worker engagement in the U.S. and globally. They define *engaged employees* as those who are involved in, enthusiastic about and committed to their work and workplace. Employee engagement in the U.S. is currently 34%, the highest level since Gallup began reporting the national figure in 2000 (this level ties March 2016, when Gallup also reported 34% of U.S. employees were engaged).

The other side of this coin is what Gallup refers to as *not engaged* and *actively disengaged* workers. According to Gallup, 13% of workers are actively disengaged - those who have miserable work experiences. The remaining 53% of workers are in the *not engaged* category, meaning psychologically unattached to their work and company. Because their engagement needs are not fully met, they're putting time, but not energy or passion, into their work. They may be generally satisfied but aren't cognitively and emotionally connected to their work. They usually show up to work and do the minimum required but will leave their company for a slightly better offer.[5]

In total, Gallup's research says a whopping 66% of all employees across all industries are either not engaged or actively disengaged from their work! Why so many disengaged workers? Gallup's engagement survey is anchored in employees' performance management needs. When those needs are met, employees become emotionally and psychologically attached to their work and workplace, and their individual performance excels. When needs are not met, engagement suffers.

Gallup's Global Workplace report[6] suggests that investing in employee development is critical. Their research found that one of the most informative survey questions – *Is there someone at work who encourages my development?* - separates enthusiastic, high-performing workers from low-performing, miserable ones. What leads to the greatest engagement and productivity? Businesses that focus on basic human needs for psychological engagement — such as positive workplace relationships, frequent recognition, ongoing performance conversations and opportunities for personal development.

As a leader, understanding what creates engagement for yourself and others is a key success factor. If you manage others, this knowledge empowers you to set a high standard of proactive relationship management and engagement with your

---

[5] https://news.gallup.com/poll/241649/employee-engagement-rise.aspx
[6] https://www.gallup.com/workplace/238079/state-global-workplace-2017.aspx

team members. If you are an individual contributor, active demonstration of *Leading from Where you Are* themes will motivate your own engagement and inspire others. Practicing the themes helps you develop stronger relationships, become more influential, and make a greater impact within the organization. Leadership is always about actions, not position.

Real Leadership

In one of my job assignments, I worked in 24-story office building in Downtown Long Beach, located less than a mile from the beach. I noticed that all the tall buildings on Ocean Boulevard were about the same height. No outliers 50 or 100 stories tall stood in that area.

One morning, a co-worker and I got coffee at a shop in the lobby of our building. I mentioned my observations to her about the common building height while we waited for our coffee. An architect who also worked in the building overheard my comment and said, "The reason no buildings are taller than this one is because a building's height is limited by the depth of its foundation. If you want to go higher, you need to dig deeper. The water table is high under this building and the soil is sandy and soft, so we can't dig any deeper."

The architect's comments provide a metaphor for real leadership. *If we want to go higher in what we accomplish, we must dig deeper within ourselves to build a stronger foundation from which to grow.* Your work environment always changes. Some industries change faster than others; all are subject to evolution or revolution. Ask yourself this question, *What will my touchstone be to stay anchored as a leader as the environment in my company and outside changes?* Said another way, *how deep is your leadership foundation today, and how much deeper will it need to be tomorrow?*

It's a matter of choice

The notion that we choose how we show up in our work, either intentionally or unconsciously, is a thread throughout this book. The root of this concept is *choice*. We can control very few things in the world, but we do choose our attitudes, priorities and behaviors. Effective leaders know success is based on making the best choices possible, all things considered. *Leading from Where you Are* prepares you with actionable themes to perform whenever you believe they fit the situation. Hold sacred those decisions you make throughout your leadership journey, and know which choices are yours to make.

Staying on track when others don't

In organizations of all sizes, there is always some type of *current* - a pull towards the mean of what is expected and acceptable. The current can flow in a positive direction, be neutral or perhaps it's a negative undercurrent. *Leading from Where you Are* means finding the most positive, optimistic path available and maintaining a disciplined commitment to intentionally manage your leadership presence even when others flow with the current.

Points of Progress

What are your milestones for success as a leader? Recognition? New assignments? Promotion? Titles? Greater compensation? Fulfilment? Whatever measure you use, the results of your investment in *Leading from Where you Are* gives you a personal experience. External recognition of progress tends to fade, so focus on intrinsic rewards when you think about the measures of success you seek.

Meaningful metrics

One of my favorite Peter Drucker sayings is *what gets measured gets managed*. This applies to our personal actions and performance as well as organizational performance. How will you evaluate yourself relative to the results you want to achieve in your leadership journey? Knowing in advance how you will define success and what milestones will represent progress matters.

See the connection between cause and effect

Effective activities precede desired results. Leaders who create meaningful results focus on effective execution of activities aligned with their areas of greatest personal impact. *Deconstructing results* will diagnose activities performed and the effectiveness of execution that created the results.

This approach to interpreting results, analyzing the specific activities which caused them, may be new to you.

A more familiar approach to analyzing performance is to view results and ask, *"How can I do better?"* The shortcoming of that traditional approach is it overlooks what *caused* the results; analogous to saying *just try harder and you'll get the results you expect.*

Patty managed a business development team in a bank wealth management group when I served as her executive coach. Karen was new to Patty's team. Karen stood out through her enthusiastic, confident approach to engaging prospective clients and deep subject matter expertise. She had what it took to be a successful business development officer, but she couldn't close a deal.

Patty was frustrated and at a loss about how to help Karen produce the results she expected. Patty and I started our analysis by deconstructing Karen's sales results. Over her first six months in the job, Karen hadn't produced any new business, so her results were $0 in sales. Then we brought Karen into the conversation and deconstructed her *activities*. What we learned was enlightening.

Karen was outstanding at identifying and meeting new prospects. She did a wonderful job developing service proposals that addressed prospects' needs. Then we found the missing link. After a prospect accepted Karen's service proposal, she dropped the ball. She was ineffective in following through completion of the bank's paperwork to set-up the new services. Karen had no problem with the hard parts of the job – finding new prospects and selling the business; she lost the deals due to her administrative challenges.

By deconstructing results and identifying their root causes, Patty helped Karen create the expected outcomes. To solve the problem, Patty assigned an administrative assistant to Karen exclusively to complete paperwork for new clients. By the end of the next month, Karen had exceeded her new business goal for the quarter.

If you deconstruct financial results in your department for the quarter, your first questions are:

- *How do these results align with our expectations?*
- *What are the activities that contributed to these results?*
- *Were we engaged in the right activities?*
- *How effectively did we perform these activities?*

Whether results exceed, fall short or meet expectations, deconstruction helps understand the root cause of the outcome. With a cause and effect understanding, you can craft plans for future activities that adjust specific actions to achieve or sustain production of desired results.

Celebrate your progress

Leadership is a process of continually evaluating the operating environment, environmental changes, your performance and identification of opportunities to adjust your approach. Find opportunities along the journey to celebrate your personal observable progress. If you've made a particularly rewarding contribution to a team meeting, take time to soak in the moment. When you hear positive feedback from a colleague or management, pause to experience the feeling. You invest time in looking for ways to refine and improve your performance and it's important to savor the benefits of your efforts.

Building and Recommitting

Effective leaders continually reinvent themselves. The *process* of leadership is accretive. Experiences build and inform the leader how to draw from previous experiences to approach the next situation while fine-tuning their repertoire. With this process mindset, effective leadership practitioners thirst for opportunities to enhance skills, re-engineer competencies, re-set markers of success and elicit feedback on how they show up.

Commitment is dedication to a cause, and your leadership journey is a worthy cause. Competing priorities can become distractions from the things we *want* to accomplish as leaders. Regular recommitment to continual growth can take the form of formal training, frequent reading or mentoring others in *Leading from Where you Are*. The goal is to stay committed to leadership as a process.

Chapter 10
Along the Path

A traditional definition of management describes four functions – *planning, organizing, leading* and *controlling*. When I studied this definition as an undergraduate student, three of these functions made sense, but the notion of *control* as a manager didn't resonate. Certainly, managers make decisions that direct activities and resources, with parameters – ethical, legal, regulatory, policy, cultural, economic - affecting those decisions. Add in the human element. Managers must define expectations of their employees, a key responsibility in carrying out activities of an organization. However, the employee holds the ultimate ability to perform to expectations or not; to stay in their job or resign.

The further I progressed in my career in management assignments and teaching strategic management, the less comfortable I became with the control concept as a function of management. As a bank executive, I frequently met with clients who achieved success in the business world. One day at lunch with a Fortune 100 CEO, we were discussing leadership, and differences between leading and managing.

I asked, "As a CEO, what do you think about the idea of control. What do you actually control in your company?" *If* control exists anywhere in an organization, it resides at the CEO's chair.

He said, "In reality, I don't control anything. The strongest tool I have available is influence. I can set policies, manage the budget and promote my agenda for the company. But I really don't control anything."

Remarkable! This successful CEO, responsible for thousands of employees and a multi-billion-dollar operation, believed influence was his most powerful resource.

As I absorbed that CEO's perspective, I tested the concept in the business I led and with other senior executives. The more C-suite executives of for profit and nonprofit organizations I asked about their ability to control things, the more I learned about the importance of influence.

From years as an executive and the wide range of conversations I had on this and broader areas of management responsibilities, my definition has evolved. The functions of management are:

- *Lead* – articulate the future state of the organization.
- *Influence* - inspire advocacy for the vision and activities required to bring it to life.
- *Listen* – be a sounding board for people who want someone to hear them – employees, customers, vendors, stakeholders.
- *Manage* – assign activities and focus resources to fulfill the vision; hold people accountable for fulfilment.
- *Coach* – serve others by helping enhance their effectiveness through self-awareness, prioritization, and clarity in identifying the role they need to play in any given circumstance.

Each of these functions are discrete, so managers must observe and understand which role they need to play in any given circumstance and adapt to meet the needs.

I managed someone who had several challenging employees on her team, all strong contributors to the company. However, three of those people were not the least bit user-friendly. In our one-to-one meetings, the manager shared the progress her team made with projects they worked through. My role was to *coach*. I asked coaching questions like, "Some of your work crosses into other departments; what level of support are you receiving from those areas to help deliver your projects?" or "Is there anything on the horizon that might make it difficult to continue progress on your projects?" or "I know you've been working on developing your presentation skills; how are you feeling about the progress you're making?"

In another one-to-one conversation, we talked about performance reviews for her team members and how her employees progressed relative to their specific objectives for the quarter. In that conversation, I needed to play the role of *manager*.

Late one afternoon, I received a call from this manager as she left an offsite meeting with her team. She was frustrated, felt down on herself about the way she dealt with one of her team members. This employee frequently got under her skin, and she felt at her wits end that afternoon. In that conversation, my role was to *listen* and support; not to manage, lead or fix anything. At other times, my role was to influence or lead with this manager.

The take-away with this definition of management is that we must *observe, interpret and adapt* to meet the needs of others and the organization as circumstances change. Throughout

116 Leading from Where You Are
116 Leading from Where You Are

your leadership journey, you face challenges and opportunities that enable you to develop, grow, fine-tune your presence and what you contribute to your organization.

When I look at my path, it seems every time I felt comfortable, something happened that snapped me into a less comfortable environment. Sometimes, changing expectations of clients, new regulations or competition drove the discomfort. Occasionally, a more urgent cause like a reorganization or merger drove it. In other cases, the discomfort came from my personal changes and growth.

From academic research and personal experience, I am certain that our path is never a straight line forward. Unexpected twists and turns always stretch us in ways we didn't think we could move. I invested much of my career working in financial services, directly in the business or as a consultant.

This industry has experienced remarkable structural change. One marker of the change is the number of participants in the industry. In the mid-1960's, the number of banks in the U.S. peaked at close to 24,000. When I was a management trainee at Bank of America in the late 1980's, that number had decreased to 14,000. Driven by regulatory and economic changes, today the number of banks in the country is 5,000.

For me, these industry dynamics presented great opportunity due to continuous changing of players in the business, rules and regulations of how firms operate, and the definition of what success looked like in each position I held. In addition to industry consolidations, I had 30 managers in the parts of my career when I worked for a bank. Considering that my longest tenure with the same manager was 15 years, the rate of change during the other years was extraordinary!

A wonderful Latin phrase gets at the essence of challenges which help us grow - *per ardua ad astra* – "through adversity to the stars." Personal development cannot take place without adversity and resistance. With physical exercise, people often focus on resistance training – using muscles to contract against an external resistance (weights) with the expectation they will increase strength and endurance. The same principle applies to leaders. Resistance is normal, and the more we work with it, anticipate it, and develop through it, the more fit we become as leaders. *Knowing* that adversity, challenges and resistance are part of the journey helps you frame your thinking.

As you navigate your leadership journey and practice the themes you've learned through *Leading from Where you Are*, I invite you to consider these additional thoughts to help you continue stretching and growing through comfortable and uncomfortable experiences. I refer to these as *leadership sustainability ideas*.

Leadership Sustainability Ideas

- *The Mirror of Truth* – Every human being has blind spots - gaps in our self-awareness that diminish our ability to accurately assess how we show up. Find trusted colleagues who help you see things in yourself you may miss. For instance, you may mismanage your time allocation – overinvest in activities that aren't productive or don't align with the mission you're pursuing. Ask for observations and don't defend yourself or try to justify your actions when you receive the feedback. Simply thank the person who cares enough to share their candid observations with you.

Also, consider seeking formal 360-degree feedback from your peers if available to you through your firm or a professional executive coach. Continually work to raise your self-awareness.

- *Brave Exploration* - Look for things you may not want to see and listen for what you may not want to hear within and around your organization. I worked at a company with a long run of great success. Then, in what felt like an *out of the blue* experience, the company temporarily fell from grace. In its simplest form, I distilled the root cause of the problems from the fact that the CEO had unwavering trust in one key leader, so he never asked her the hard questions he might not like to hear answered. Inappropriate activities took place in her division. He was largely unaware of the impact or long-term consequences to the business. By avoiding Brave Exploration, he lost his job and caused the company years of pain.

- *Solution Developer* – People who are *problem identifiers* amply populate organizations. Seeing an issue isn't a particularly unique talent. Committing to developing solutions is a valuable discipline. In occasional cases, no time exists between issue identification and when the situation needs to be communicated. Being a solution developer means, in those cases where there is time following issue identification, you facilitate ideation about potential solutions to accompany conversations around the problem.

- *Connection Recognition* – The larger your organization, the more complex and multifaceted it becomes. A byproduct of complexity can be that it becomes easy to miss connections across departments, divisions or operating entities. When you are in a position that enables you to see issues or opportunities others may be missing, draw from your *Leading from Where you Are* competencies to communicate with others who can address or own the situation. The essence of this idea is to identify opportunities to contribute to change, regardless of where in the organization the need resides. This doesn't assume your input is always invited, or even appreciated. However, the risk of not offering ideas that can benefit or protect the organization usually exceeds that of sharing observations which can lead to improvement.

- *Always be on Message* – A fundamental principle of *Leading from Where you Are* is *intentional communication*. A saying intended to guide politicians says, "The microphone is always on." It stems from the many unfortunate gaffs made when politicians say something they shouldn't, and their comment is picked up on a hot mic then shared broadly. In context of *leadership sustainability*, always remain mindful of what you say, your choice of words and tone to assure people see you the way you want to be seen. It's much easier to manage your message continually than to do damage control later.

- *Pragmatism over Perfection* – This is easier for some people than others. Determine the optimal level of input into a project or assignment to generate the best outcome, and don't overinvest in tasks that won't make a difference. If perfection is the standard for a task, so be it; if a task has a different standard, don't overengineer the solution.

- *Propel Optimism* – Optimism is contagious, an essential ingredient in leadership, because people always watch leaders to set the tone. Winston Churchill once said, "A pessimist sees the difficulty in every opportunity; an optimist sees the opportunity in every difficulty." Optimism is *not* a substitute for realism, candor or clarity about the reality in which you operate; it's not Pollyanna. It is a mindset which reflects a positive expectancy that things will work out favorably.

- *Own a Critical Few Priorities* – Jim Collins, author of *Good to Great* says that if you have more than three priorities, you don't have any priorities. In his book *Great at Work*, Mort Hansen encourages people to *do less and obsess*. Hansen says to work smart means to maximize the value of your work by selecting a few activities and applying intense targeted effort. While everything in your work is important, not everything is a priority. Determine what your critical few priorities are – those activities where you can make the greatest impact and contribute to the most meaningful results, then disproportionately invest in what it takes to accomplish them.

- *Take Comfort in Autonomy* – Leaders exist to serve others. When you practice themes from *Leading from Where you Are*, the goal is bettering the organization though your contributions. Occasionally, you will receive recognition, which feels good. Most of the time you won't get recognition. Add to this the importance as a leader of highlighting the people you work with or who report to you, and you will recognize that *it's not about you!* One of my favorite commentaries on leadership is from the 4th century B.C. Tao Te Ching. The 17th verse says:

The greatest type of leader is one of whose existence
the people are hardly aware.
Next best is a leader who is loved and praised.
Next comes the one who is feared.
The worst is the one who is despised.

When a leader doesn't trust the people,
they will become untrustworthy.

The best leader speaks little.
He never speaks carelessly.
He works without self interest
and leaves no trace.
When the work is accomplished, the people say: "Amazing: we did it all by ourselves."

There is great strength in being a leader who guides people to results which they can own and in which they can take pride. This requires taking comfort in autonomy.

- *Renewal* – Sustainable leadership requires that we refresh ourselves through continuous learning, personal development, decompression and regular refocusing. This is the private work, acting from the inside out, to regularly recharge and be at your best.

Closing Thoughts

Leadership is a set of conscious choices and behaviors, not a job title. The opportunity to lead people carries great responsibility. Through practicing the themes discussed in this book, you can enhance the meaningfulness of your work and effectively manage the responsibility of leadership. My hope is that as you practice these themes, you experience greater fulfilment, enjoyment and success in your work, *Leading from Where you Are.*

Made in the USA
Coppell, TX
30 October 2020